LIFE BY THE NUMBERS
Quotations You Can Count On

David Jouris

Illustrations by John Grimes

**Andrews McMeel
Publishing**

Kansas City

01 02 03 04 05 WLS 10 9 8 7 6 5 4 3 2 1

ISBN: 0-7407-1896-7

Library of Congress Catalog Card Number: 2001086434

Book design by Holly Camerlinck
Illustrations © 2001 by John Grimes (john@grimescartoons.com)

Attention: Schools and Businesses

Andrews McMeel books are available at quantity discounts with bulk purchase for educational, business, or sales promotional use. For information, please write to: Special Sales Department, Andrews McMeel Publishing, 4520 Main Street, Kansas City, Missouri 64111.

For my mother and father

INTRODUCTION

None of us really understands
what's going on with all these numbers.

— DAVID STOCKMAN, FORMER DIRECTOR OF THE
OFFICE OF MANAGEMENT AND BUDGET

I have been keeping my eyes and ears open for interesting quotations for
quite a few years now. (I've also been keeping my mouth open, but
that's for a cookbook project.) It started when I was gathering quotations that could be used to introduce a wide variety of subjects in an
atlas of thematic maps I'd created. However, as with so many things,
the collection expanded beyond the original concept and took on a
life of its own.

To keep some semblance of order, I divided my ever-expanding quotation list into major groupings that particularly intrigued me. Among the first categories I began to focus on were quotations involving numbers—"There are two kinds of people in this world . . . ," "The three most important things in life are . . . ," etc.—and I began to build a file for each number from one to ten.

There are, it turns out, a great many quotations involving the numbers two and three; noticeably fewer use the numbers one and four. Beyond four, the amount of quotations drops so dramatically that there was no point in having separate files for them.

For the record, the quotations in this collection were gathered from a variety of sources, including newspapers, magazines, books, movies, television, radio, and the Internet. The book further benefited greatly from the assistance of numerous friends, both in America and abroad. And some of the lines I've included here came from that most wonderful of all reference tools—the quotation books.

ONES

We always take care of number one.

— FREDERICK MARRYAT

There's one way to find out if a man is honest: ask him;
if he says yes, you know he is crooked.

— GROUCHO MARX

The only honest art form is laughter. You can't fake it.

— LENNY BRUCE

There is only one honest impulse at the bottom of Puritanism,
and that is the impulse to punish the man
with a superior capacity for happiness.

— H. L. MENCKEN

There is only one way to happiness and that is to cease worrying
about things which are beyond the power of our will.

— EPICTETUS

There is only one way to achieve happiness on this terrestrial ball.
And that is to have a clear conscience, or none at all.

—OGDEN NASH

There is only one passion, the passion for happiness.

—DENIS DIDEROT

There is only one happiness in life: to love and be loved.

—GEORGE SAND

All the unhappiness of man stems from one thing only:
that he is incapable of staying quietly in his room.

—BLAISE PASCAL

There are many ways of going forward, but only one way of standing still.

— FRANKLIN D. ROOSEVELT

There is one quality that characterizes all of us who deal with the sciences of the earth and its life — we are never bored.

— RACHEL CARSON

The politicians have one basic remedy for boredom and this is war or revolution.

— ISAAC BASHEVIS SINGER

There is only one decisive victory: the last.

— KARL VON CLAUSEWITZ

The only way to abolish war is to make peace heroic.

— JOHN DEWEY

The foreign policy of America can best be described by one word — peace.

— CALVIN COOLIDGE

They know only one word of more than one syllable here,
and that is *fillum*.

— LOUIS SHERWIN, ON HOLLYWOOD

There is only one cure for the evils
which newly acquired freedom produces; and that cure is freedom.

— LORD THOMAS MACAULAY

Liberty is the one thing you can't have unless you give it to others.

— WILLIAM ALLEN WHITE

The only cure for loneliness is solitude.

— MARIANNE MOORE

There is only one cure for gray hair. It was invented by a Frenchman. It is called the guillotine.

—P. G. WODEHOUSE

If you have formed the habit of checking on every new diet that comes along, you will find that, mercifully, they all blur together, leaving you with only one definite piece of information: french-fried potatoes are out.

—JEAN KERR

There was only one occasion in my life when I put myself on a strict diet and I can tell you, hand on heart, it was the most miserable afternoon I have ever spent.

—DENIS NORDEN

There is only one big thing—desire. And before it, when it is big, all is little.

—WILLA CATHER

In my experience, there is only one motivation, and that is desire.
No reasons or principles contain it or stand against it.

— JANE SMILEY

Only passions, great passions, can elevate the soul to great things.

— DENIS DIDEROT

The only sin passion can commit is to be joyless.

— DOROTHY L. SAYERS

Cruelty is the only sin.

— ELLEN GLASGOW

The only sin is mediocrity.

— MARTHA GRAHAM

The only deadly sin I know is cynicism.

— HENRY LEWIS STIMSON

There's only one real sin, and that is to persuade oneself
that the second-best is anything but the second-best.

— DORIS LESSING

The only sin which we never forgive in each other
is difference of opinion.

— RALPH WALDO EMERSON

The only truth lies in learning to free ourselves
from insane passion for truth.

— UMBERTO ECO

I believe that truth has only one face:
that of a violent contradiction.

—GEORGES BATAILLE

There is only one thing a philosopher can be relied upon to do,
and that is to contradict other philosophers.

— WILLIAM JAMES

There is only one thing that requires real courage to say,
and that is a truism.

— G. K. CHESTERTON

There is only one real failure in life that is possible,
and that is not to be true to the best one knows.

— FREDERICK WILLIAM FARRAR

Only the truth can still astonish people.

— JEAN-MARIE POUPART

Truth is the only safe ground to stand upon.

—ELIZABETH CADY STANTON

Fantasy is the only truth.

—ABBIE HOFFMAN

There's only one answer to a lie, and that's the truth.

—WILLIAM J. DONOVAN

The truth is that there is only one terminal dignity—love.
And the story of a love is not important—
what is important is that one is capable of love.

—HELEN HAYES

The only way to speak the truth is to speak lovingly.

—HENRY DAVID THOREAU

There is only one "damage control"—and that's the truth.

— BEN BRADLEE

Advertisements contain the only truths to be relied on in a newspaper.

— THOMAS JEFFERSON

The only thing you can believe in a newspaper is the date.

— J. B. S. HALDANE

There is but one way for a newspaperman to look at a politician, and that is down.

— FRANK H. SIMONDS

The only intelligent way to discuss politics is on all fours.

— TIMOTHY LEARY

As a poet there is only one political duty—
and that is to defend one's language from corruption.

—W. H. AUDEN

There is only one political career for which women
are perfectly suitable—diplomacy.

—CLARE BOOTHE LUCE

The only way to cut government spending
is not to give them the money to spend in the first place.

—HOWARD JARVIS

The only absolutely safe way to double your money
is to fold it once and put it in your pocket.

—FRANK MCKINNEY HUBBARD

Divorce is the one human tragedy that reduces everything to cash.
— RITA MAE BROWN

The universal regard for money is the one hopeful fact in our civilization.
— GEORGE BERNARD SHAW

Tolerance is the only real test of civilization.
— SIR ARTHUR HELPS

If there be one test of national genius universally accepted, it is success.
— RALPH WALDO EMERSON

The only worthy response to danger and failure
is a renewed dedication to success.
— ADLAI STEVENSON

The vital, successful people I have met all had
one common characteristic. They had a plan.

— MARILYN VAN DERBUR

All the successful parents I have observed seem to possess
one common quality: that of being able to visit with their children.

— MARCELENE COX

There's only one way to succeed in anything,
and that is to give it everything.

— VINCE LOMBARDI

The one predominant duty is to find one's work and do it.

— CHARLOTTE PERKINS GILMAN

It's one of the tragic ironies of the theatre that only one man in it
can count on steady work—the night watchman.

—TALLULAH BANKHEAD

There is only one thing people like that is good for them:
a good night's sleep.

—EDGAR WATSON HOWE

The only thing you owe the public is a good performance.

—HUMPHREY BOGART

Only the gentle are ever really strong.

—JAMES DEAN

There is one thing stronger than all the armies in the world:
an idea whose time has come.

—VICTOR HUGO

The weak have one weapon: the errors of those who think they are strong.

— GEORGES BIDAULT

The only weapon against bad ideas is better ideas.

— ALFRED WHITNEY GRISWOLD

Democracy is the best system of government yet devised, but it suffers from one great defect — it does not encourage those military virtues upon which, in an envious world, it must frequently depend for survival.

— GUY DU MAURIER

If there is one basic element in our Constitution it is civilian control of the military.

— HARRY S TRUMAN

There is only one basic human right, the right to do as you damn well please. And with it comes the only basic human duty, the duty to take the consequences.

— P. J. O'Rourke

There's only one length for a story and that's the right length.

— Alfred W. Stewart

It is only with the heart that one can see rightly; what is essential is invisible to the eye.

— Antoine de Saint-Exupéry

The only thing that makes one place more attractive to me than another is the quantity of heart I find in it.

— Jane Welsh Carlyle

Travel is glamorous only in retrospect.

—Paul Theroux

The only country in the world where failing to promote yourself
is regarded as being arrogant.

— GARRY TRUDEAU, ON THE UNITED STATES

There is only one thing in the world worse than being talked about,
and that is not being talked about.

— OSCAR WILDE

The only joy in the world is to begin.

— CESARE PAVESE

There's only one person in the whole world like you,
and that's you yourself.

— FRED ROGERS

The only factor becoming scarce in a world of abundance
is human attention.

— KEVIN KELLY

The only thing that can save the world is the reclaiming
of the awareness of the world. That's what poetry does.

— ALLEN GINSBERG

The only thing that saves us from the bureaucracy is inefficiency.

— EUGENE MCCARTHY

The only thing that makes life possible is permanent,
intolerable uncertainty: not knowing what comes next.

— URSULA LEGUIN

There is one thing certain, namely, that we can have nothing certain;
therefore it is not certain that we can have nothing certain.

— SAMUEL BUTLER

There's only one corner of the universe you can be certain of improving,
and that's your own self.

— ALDOUS HUXLEY

There is only one valuable thing in art:
the thing you cannot explain.

— GEORGES BRAQUE

There's only one way to know about art: through exposure.

— JEAN SUTHERLAND BOGGS

Every work of art has one indispensable mark . . . the centre of it is simple, however much the fulfillment may be complicated.

— G. K. CHESTERTON

The enjoyment of art is the only remaining ecstasy that's neither immoral nor illegal.

— CLIFTON WEBB

The one universal form of art is music.

— FAITH BALDWIN

Art is the only way to run away without leaving home.

— TWYLA THARP

The only way of discovering the limits of the possible
is to venture a little way past them into the impossible.

—ARTHUR C. CLARKE

One thing we know beyond all doubt: Nothing has ever
been achieved by the person who says, "It can't be done."

—ELEANOR ROOSEVELT

There is only one admirable form of the imagination: the imagination that
is so intense that it creates a new reality, that it makes things happen,
whether it be a political thing, or a social thing or a work of art.

—SEÁN O'FAOLÁIN

Take only your imagination seriously.

—THOMAS BERGER

There are things that are so serious that you can only joke about them.

— WERNER HEISENBERG

If there's one thing I hate more than not being taken seriously,
it's being taken too seriously.

— BILLY WILDER

Seriousness is the only refuge of the shallow.

— OSCAR WILDE

There is but one truly serious philosophical problem, and that is suicide.

— ALBERT CAMUS

People commit suicide for only one reason — to escape torment.

— LI ANG

There ain't but one time to go fishin' and that's whenever you can.
— DIRON TALBERT

Learning learns but one lesson: doubt!
— GEORGE BERNARD SHAW

There is but one step from the grotesque to the horrible.
— SIR ARTHUR CONAN DOYLE

From the sublime to the ridiculous there is but one step.
— NAPOLEON BONAPARTE

From fanaticism to barbarism is only one step.
— DENIS DIDEROT

It is only one step from toleration to forgiveness.

—SIR ARTHUR WING PINERO

Guilt is the one burden human beings can't bear alone.

—ANAÏS NIN

There's one thing worse than being alone: wishing you were.

—BOB STEELE

There's one thing to be said for inviting trouble: It generally accepts.

—MAY MALOO

The one thing that doesn't abide by majority rule is a person's conscience.

—HARPER LEE

There is one thing every consultant should know:
the key, I repeat, the key to consulting
is effective use of metaphor.

—KEN ROCK

There is only one thing that there isn't—and that's oblivion.

—JORGE LUIS BORGES

There is only one protection against destiny: nothingness.

—FRIEDRICH HEBBEL

The inevitable is the one thing I invariably accept.

—ERNEST BRAMAH

Good manners spring from just one thing—kind impulses.

—ELSA MAXWELL

There is one thing alone that stands the brunt of life
throughout its course, a quiet conscience.

—EURIPIDES

One must bear in mind one thing.
It isn't necessary to know what that thing is.

—JOHN ASHBERRY

The only thing that matters is experience.

—MICHELANGELO ANTONIONI

The only thing we have to fear is fear itself.

—FRANKLIN D. ROOSEVELT

The one permanent emotion of the inferior man, as of all the simpler mammals, is fear—fear of the unknown, the complex, the inexplicable.

—H. L. MENCKEN

The one mystery we shall never solve is the enigma of human identity.

—EMLYN WILLIAMS

There is one spectacle grander than the sea, that is the sky;
there is one spectacle grander than the sky, that is the interior of the soul.

—VICTOR HUGO

Misquotations are the only quotations that are never misquoted.

—HESKETH PEARSON

The only one who makes no mistakes is one who never does anything!

—THEODORE ROOSEVELT

Perfection has one grave defect: it is apt to be dull.

—W. SOMERSET MAUGHAM

I have a theory that the only original things we ever do are mistakes.

—BILLY JOEL

The one thing that the public dislike is novelty.

— OSCAR WILDE

Originality is the one thing which un-original minds cannot feel the use of.

— JOHN STUART MILL

The only real elegance is in the mind.
If you've got that, the rest really follows from it.

— DIANA VREELAND

There is only one situation I can think of in which men and women
make an effort to read better than they usually do . . .
when they are in love and reading a love letter.

— MORTIMER ADLER

Letter-writing is the only device for combining solitude and good company.

— LORD BYRON

The only critics worth reading are the critics who practice,
and practice well, the art of which they write.

— T. S. ELIOT

There is only one trait that marks the writer. He is always watching.

— MORLEY CALLAGHAN

Writing is the only profession where no one considers you ridiculous
if you earn no money.

— JULES RENARD

There is only one way to defeat the enemy, and that is to write
as well as one can. The best argument is an undeniably good book.

— SAUL BELLOW

I have learned in my 30-odd years of serious writing only one sure lesson:
Stories, like whiskey, must be allowed to mature in the cask.

— SEÁN O'FAOLÁIN

All good books have one thing in common.
They are truer than if they had really happened.

— ERNEST HEMINGWAY

The only obligation to which in advance we may hold a novel, without
incurring the accusation of being arbitrary, is that it be interesting.

— HENRY JAMES

It is only in literature that coincidences seem unnatural.

— ROBERT LYND

There are several kinds of stories, but only one difficult kind —
the humorous.

— MARK TWAIN

The poet's only responsibility is to write fresh lines.

— CHARLES OLSON

The only way I can figure out what I really think
about anything is to write about it.

— NORMAN MAILER

There are no evil thoughts except one: the refusal to think.

— AYN RAND

The only reason some people get lost in thought
is because it's unfamiliar territory.

— PAUL FIX

Curiosity is the one thing invincible in Nature.

— FREYA STARK

There is always one moment in childhood
when the door opens and lets in the future.

— GRAHAM GREENE

Youth has one great element in its favor—it can live in the future.

— HENRY FORD

The only certainty in the remote future is that
radically new things will be happening.

— FREEMAN DYSON

The only reason people want to be masters of the future
is to change the past.

— MILAN KUNDERA

There is only one way left to escape the alienation of present day society:
to retreat ahead of it.

— ROLAND BARTHES

There is one, and only one, thing in modern society
more hideous than crime — namely, repressive justice.

— SIMONE WEIL

I have come to believe that the one thing people cannot bear
is a sense of injustice.

— MILICENT FENWICK

Law school taught me one thing: how to take two situations
that are exactly the same and show how they are different.

— HART POMERANTZ

There is one kind of robber whom the law does not strike at,
and who steals what is most precious to men: time.

— NAPOLEON BONAPARTE

Motorists have exhibited the one worse attitude than defiance of law —
indifference to it.

— FREDERICK DWIGHT

The one thing that unites all human beings, regardless of age,
gender, religion or ethnic background, is that we all believe
we are above-average drivers.

— DAVE BARRY

You can only perceive real beauty in a person as they get older.

—ANOUK AIMÉE

The only medicine for suffering, crime, and
all the other woes of mankind, is wisdom.

—THOMAS H. HUXLEY

There is one message I would give to young doctors and
that is that the goal of medicine is not to prolong life.
It is to alleviate suffering and improve the quality of life.

—CHRISTIAAN BARNARD

Man is the only animal that suffers from the disease
of self-hatred and self-contempt.

—MICHEL EYGUEM DE MONTAIGNE

There is only one proved method of assisting the advancement
of pure science—that of picking men of genius, backing them heavily,
and leaving them to direct themselves.

—JAMES B. CONANT

Words, I think, are the one great exhaustless charm and resource of life.

—GAMALIEL BRADFORD

You just have to *go on* when it is worst and most helpless—
there is only one thing to do with a novel and that is go
straight on through to the end of the damn thing.

—ERNEST HEMINGWAY

Any author writes only one book in his life.

—JEAN RENOIR

There's one good kind of a writer—a dead writer.

—JAMES T. FARRELL

The only completely consistent people are the dead.

—ALDOUS HUXLEY

Inconsistency is the only thing in which men are consistent.

—HORATIO SMITH

There is only one difference between a long life and a good dinner:
that, in the dinner, the sweets come last.

—ROBERT LOUIS STEVENSON

The only good thing about it is you're not dead.

—ATTRIBUTED TO LILLIAN HELLMAN, ON AGING

Death has but one terror—that it has no tomorrow.

—ERIC HOFFER

I have only one curiosity left: death.

—COCO CHANEL

Dying is man's only natural act.

—JACQUES BREL

Death is the only pure, beautiful conclusion of a great passion.

—D. H. LAWRENCE

The only religious way to think of death is as part and parcel of life.
—THOMAS MANN

There is only one religion, though there are a hundred versions of it.
—GEORGE BERNARD SHAW

The only man who wasn't spoiled by being lionized was Daniel.
—SIR H. BEERBOHM TREE

All religions die of one disease, that of being found out.
—JOHN MORLEY

The one certain way for a woman to hold a man is to leave him for religion.
—MURIEL SPARK

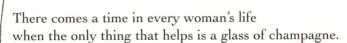

There comes a time in every woman's life
when the only thing that helps is a glass of champagne.

— BETTE DAVIS

There is one thing I know I shall never get enough of—champagne.

—M. F. K. Fisher

The one thing we can never get enough of is love.
And the one thing we never give enough is love.

—Henry Miller

Only the bold have good luck in love.

—Carlo Goldoni

I know of only one duty, and that is to love.

—Albert Camus

There is only one real deprivation, I decided this morning,
and that is not to be able to give one's gifts to those one loves most.

—May Sarton

If you can give your son or daughter only one gift, let it be enthusiasm.

— BRUCE BARTON

One word frees us of all the weight and pain of life: That word is love.

— SOPHOCLES

There is only one thing that arouses animals more than pleasure,
and that is pain.

— UMBERTO ECO

Speed provides the one genuinely modern pleasure.

— ALDOUS HUXLEY

There is only one genuine misfortune: not to be born.

— JOAQUIM MARIS MACHADO DE ASSIS

To give birth to form is the only act of man that has any consequence.

— CLAES OLDENBURG

The only form of lying that is absolutely beyond reproach
is lying for its own sake.

— OSCAR WILDE

There are 869 different forms of lying,
but only one of them has been squarely forbidden.
Thou shalt not bear false witness against thy neighbor.

— MARK TWAIN

There is only one blasphemy, and that is the refusal to experience joy.

— PAUL RUDNICK

All joys I bless, but I confess
There is one greatest thrill:
What the dentist does
When he stops the buzz
And puts away the drill.

— CHRISTOPHER MORLEY

There is only one answer to destructiveness and that is creativity.

— SYLVIA ASHTON-WARNER

The only alternative to co-existence is co-destruction.

— JAWAHARLAL NEHRU

When you appeal to force, there's one thing you must never do—lose.

— DWIGHT D. EISENHOWER

There is only one thing which I hate more than piety,
and that is patriotism.

— CHARLES BABBAGE

The only way to get the best of an argument is to avoid it.

— DALE CARNEGIE

There is only one tactical principle which is not subject to change.
It is: to use the means at hand to inflict the maximum amount of wounds,
death and destruction on the enemy in the minimum of time.

— GEORGE S. PATTON, JR.

Once a government is committed to the principle of silencing the voice
of opposition, it has only one way to go, and that is down the path of
increasingly repressive measures, until it becomes a source of terror
to all its citizens and creates a country where everyone lives in fear.

— HARRY S TRUMAN

The only people who should be in government are those who
care more about people than they do about power.

—MILLICENT FENWICK

Power has only one duty—to secure the social welfare of the People.

—BENJAMIN DISRAELI

The one power a man has that cannot be stripped from him
is the power to do nothing.

—MORGAN LLYWELYN

The only limits of power are the bounds of belief.

—HAROLD WILSON

There is only one time that is important—NOW! It is the most
important time because it is the only time that we have any power.

—LEO TOLSTOY

The only time to believe any kind of rating
is when it shows you at the top.

—BOB HOPE

The one fact that I would cry from every housetop is this:
the Good Life is waiting for us—here and now!

—B. F. SKINNER

The only good government is a bad one in the hell of a fright.

—JOYCE CARY

There is one thing better than good government,
and that is government in which all people have a part.

—WALTER HINES PAGE

The only thing necessary for the triumph of evil
is for enough good men to do nothing.

—ATTRIBUTED TO EDMUND BURKE

The one pervading evil of democracy is the tyranny of the majority,
or rather of that party, not always the majority, that succeeds,
by force or fraud, in carrying elections.

—JOHN EMERICH DALBERG-ACTON

There is only one good, knowledge, and one evil, ignorance.

—SOCRATES

The one prudence of life is concentration; the one evil is dissipation.

—RALPH WALDO EMERSON

The one important thing in life is to see to it that you are never beaten.

— ANDRÉ MALRAUX

If you could choose one characteristic that would get you through life,
choose a sense of humor.

— JENNIFER JONES

The only thing worth having in an earthly existence is a sense of humor.

— LINCOLN STEFFENS

A man has only one way of being immortal on this earth:
he has to forget he is a mortal.

— JEAN GIRAUDOUX

A ghetto can be improved in one way only: out of existence.

— JAMES BALDWIN

There is only one way to endure man's inhumanity to man and that is to try, in one's own life, to exemplify man's humanity to man.

—ALAN PATON

There is only one way to treat a cold, and that is with contempt.

—SIR WILLIAM OSLER

The one way to get thin is to re-establish a purpose in life.

—CYRIL CONNOLLY

The only way to be sure of catching a train is to miss the one before it.

—G. K. CHESTERTON

The only way to make a man trustworthy is to trust him.

—HENRY LEWIS STIMSON

The only way to get rid of temptation is to yield to it.
— OSCAR WILDE

The only way to be absolutely safe is never to try anything for the first time.
— DR. MAGNUS PYKE

There is only one duty, only one safe course, and that is to try to be right.
— WINSTON CHURCHILL

There is but one safe thing for the vanquished: not to hope for safety.
— VIRGIL

There can only be one winner, but isn't that the American way.
— GIG YOUNG

All modern American literature comes from one book
by Mark Twain called *Huckleberry Finn*.

— ERNEST HEMINGWAY

There's only one issue and only one story. The issue is self-forgiveness
and the story is *A Christmas Carol*. Self-forgiveness takes care of all the
other issues and if you can live like Scrooge on Christmas morning,
you don't need to hear another story to remind you how to live your life.

— BILLY GOODMAN

There is only one story of our lives and we tell it over and over again,
in a thousand different disguises, whether we know it or not.

— PAM HOUSTON

There's only one way to have a happy marriage,
and as soon as I learn what it is I'll get married again.

— CLINT EASTWOOD

An easy-going husband is the one indispensable comfort of life.

—OUIDA

No human being can destroy the structure of a marriage except the two who made it. It is the one human edifice that is impregnable except from within.

—GWEN BRISTOW

There is but one honest limit to the rights of a sentient being; it is where they touch the rights of another sentient being.

—FRANCES WRIGHT

There is only one road to true human greatness: through the school of hard knocks.

—ALBERT EINSTEIN

Activity is the only road to knowledge.

— GEORGE BERNARD SHAW

The only certain knowledge is the inspired guess.

— HENRY KITCHELL WEBSTER

There's only one effectively redemptive sacrifice,
the sacrifice of self-will to make room for the knowledge of God.

— ALDOUS HUXLEY

Of all God's creatures there is only one that cannot be made the slave
of the lash. That one is the cat.

— MARK TWAIN

Only one thing is impossible for God:
to find any sense in any copyright law on the planet.

— MARK TWAIN

There is only one right form for a story
and if you fail to find that form the story will not tell itself.

— MARK TWAIN

Be aware that there is only one right way to shake hands —
a firm clasp of the other person's *whole* hand (never just a few fingers)
in a brief downward motion — no pumping, please.

— JULIA KNOWLES

Life has only one real charm — the charm of *gambling*.

— CHARLES BAUDELAIRE

There is only one success—to be able to spend your life in your own way.
— CHRISTOPHER MORLEY

The only thing that happens overnight is recognition. Not talent.
— CAROL HANEY

The only thing you have to worry about is bad luck.
— HARRY S TRUMAN

The only sure thing about luck is that it will change.
— WILSON MIZNER

Men don't change. The only thing new in the world
is the history you don't know.
— HARRY S TRUMAN

There is only one history of any importance,
and it is the history of what you once believed in,
and the history of what you came to believe in.

— KAY BOYLE

The one duty we owe to history is to rewrite it.

— OSCAR WILDE

Biography is the only true history.

— THOMAS CARLYLE

The Visionary is the only true realist.

— FEDERICO FELLINI

The wealth of the soul is the only true wealth.

— LUCIAN

In a terrible crisis there is only one element more helpless than the poor, and that is the rich.

— CLARENCE DARROW

There's only one thing money won't buy, and that's poverty.

— JOE E. LEWIS

The only language that corporations understand is money.

— CHARLES NESSON

The only immorality is not to do what one has to do when one has to do it.

— JEAN ANOUILH

The only reward of virtue is virtue; the only way to have a friend is to be one.

— RALPH WALDO EMERSON

The only sense that is common in the long run, is the sense of change, and we all instinctively avoid it.

—E. B. White

The fool has one great advantage over a man of sense—
he is always satisfied with himself.

—Napoleon Bonaparte

There is only one great cause for remorse—
to have failed to look after one's own interests.

—Italo Svevo

There is one topic peremptorily forbidden to all well-bred, to all rational mortals, namely, their distempers. If you have not slept, or if you have slept, or if you have headache, or sciatica, or leprosy, or thunder-stroke, I beseech you, by all angels, to hold your peace.

—Ralph Waldo Emerson

TWOS

To make a dream come true,
just takes two.

—William Stevenson and Sylvia Moy,
"It Takes Two"

I only take a drink on two occasions —
when I'm thirsty and when I'm not.

— BRENDAN BEHAN

Two reasons for drinking: one is, when you are thirsty, to cure it;
the other, when you are not thirsty, to prevent it.

— THOMAS LOVE PEACOCK

There are two classes of travel in America:
Steerage and Steerage with Free Drinks.
You pay a great deal extra for the free drinks, of course.

— JUDITH MARTIN

In America there are two classes of travel — first and with children.

— ROBERT BENCHLEY

There are only two classes—first class and no class.

—DAVID O. SELZNICK

There are two classes of people
who tell what is going to happen in the future:
Those who don't know, and those who don't know they don't know.

—JOHN KENNETH GALBRAITH

Only two classes of books are of universal appeal.
The very best and the very worst.

—FORD MADDOX FORD

I divide all readers into two classes:
those who read to remember and those who read to forget.

—WILLIAM LYON PHELPS

All books are divisible into two classes:
the books of the hour, and the books of all time.

— JOHN RUSKIN

There are two classes of poets — the poets by education and practice,
these we respect; and poets by nature, these we love.

— RALPH WALDO EMERSON

There may be said to be two classes of people in the world:
those who constantly divide the people of the world into two classes
and those who do not.

— ROBERT BENCHLEY

There are only two classes of people: the magnanimous and the rest.

— MARCEL PROUST

Society is divided into two classes: the shearers and the shorn;
we should always be with the former against the latter.

— CHARLES DE TALLEYRAND

People can be divided into two classes:
those who go ahead and do something, and those who sit still
and inquire, "Why wasn't it done the other way?"

— OLIVER WENDELL HOLMES

Failures are divided into two classes—those who thought and never did,
and those who did and never thought.

— JOHN CHARLES SALAK

Yes and *no* are the oldest and simplest words,
but they require the most thought.

— PYTHAGORAS

I believe the two greatest words in the English language are "play ball."

— MATT WILLIAMS

The two most beautiful words in the English language are "check enclosed."

— DOROTHY PARKER

Summer afternoon—summer afternoon; to me those have always been the two most beautiful words in the English language.

— HENRY JAMES

The two most challenging words to a screenwriter are: fade in.

— JODIE FOSTER

What I like about Hollywood is that one can get along
by knowing two words of English — *swell* and *lousy*.

— ATTRIBUTED TO VICKI BAUM

I'll give you my whole theory of directing in two words — final cut.

— ROD STEIGER

In two words: *im possible.*

— SAMUEL GOLDWYN

All philosophy lies in two words, sustain and abstain.

— EPICTETUS

All human wisdom is summed up in two words — wait and hope.

— ALEXANDRE DUMAS, PÈRE

In hunting there are but two words about safety.
Should this in the least concern you, the words are: Don't hunt.

—J. P. DONLEAVY

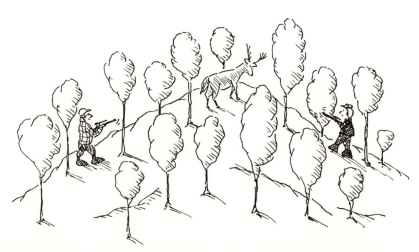

The world is made up of two classes—the hunters and the hunted.

—RICHARD CONNELL

Widows are divided into two classes—the bereaved and relieved.

—DR. VICTOR ROBINSON

There are two classes of men: those who are good with metaphors and those who are good with formulas.

—HEINRICH VON KLEIST

There are only two classes who, as categories, have courage in war— the front-line soldier and the conscientious objector.

—BASIL HENRY LIDDELL HART

All of the things in the world can be divided into two basic categories: natural things and artificial things. Or, as they are more familiarly known, nature and art.

— FRAN LEBOWITZ

There are two kinds of artists left: those who endorse Pepsi and those who simply won't.

— ANNIE LENNOX

There seem to be two causes of the deterioration of the arts: wealth and poverty.

— PLATO

Every great work of art has two faces: one toward its own time and one toward the future, toward eternity.

— DANIEL BARENBOIM

For every man there are two times that are inescapable—
the time of birth and the time of death.

— SALAH ADDOUN

I had reasoned this out in my mind, there was two things I had a right to,
liberty and death. If I could not have one, I would have the other,
for no man should take me alive.

— HARRIET TUBMAN

There are two kinds of directors in the theatre.
Those who think they are God and those who are certain of it.

— RHETTA HUGHES

There are two kinds of people: those who say to God:
"Thy will be done," and those to whom God says,
"All right, then, have it your way."

— C. S. LEWIS

Only two of God's creatures, the dog and the guitar,
have taken all sizes and shapes so as not to be separated from man.

— ANDRÉS SEGOVIA

I know two kinds of audience only — one coughing and one not coughing.

— ARTUR SCHNABEL

I occasionally play works by contemporary composers and
for two reasons. First to discourage the composer from writing any
more and secondly to remind myself how much I appreciate Beethoven.

— JASCHA HEIFETZ

There are two kinds of music — good music and bad music. Good music
is music that I want to hear. Bad music is music that I don't want to hear.

— FRAN LEBOWITZ

There's only two ways to sum up music: either it's good or it's bad.
If it's good you don't mess about with it, you just enjoy it.

— LOUIS ARMSTRONG

There are two instruments worse than a clarionet — two clarionets.

— AMBROSE BIERCE

Fear and hope are the two great instruments for the governance of men.

— JEAN-JACQUES ROUSSEAU

There are only two emotions in Wall Street: fear and greed.

— WILLIAM LE FEVRE

There are two reasons why people fail.
One is irresponsibility. The second is fear.

— WALLY AMOS

The two great movers of the human mind are the desire of good, and the fear of evil.

—Samuel Johnson

There are two levers for moving men—interest and fear.

—Napoleon Bonaparte

I am still of the opinion that only two topics can be of the least interest to a serious and studious mind—sex and the dead.

—William Butler Yeats

I think there are two areas where new ideas are terribly dangerous: economics and sex. By and large, it's all been tried, and if it's new, it's probably illegal or dangerous or unhealthy.

—Felix G. Rohatyn

There are two things that are virtually impossible
to do well in movies—prayer and sex.

—ATTRIBUTED TO ORSON WELLES

There are two thing in life one must never refuse.
One is sex and the other is television.

—GORE VIDAL

There are only two certain aphrodisiacs: (1) The presence of
an attractive woman. (2) The absence of an attractive woman.

—CLIFTON FADIMAN

When will the world know that peace and propagation
are the two most delightful things in it?

—HORACE WALPOLE

Natural man has only two primal passions: to get and to beget.

— SIR WILLIAM OSLER

When people are unhappy with their love lives, one of two things
is usually missing: passion which makes a relationship exciting,
or tenderness which makes it comforting.

— DAVID WALLIN

A traitor needs two things . . . somebody to hate, and somebody to love.

— JOHN LE CARRÉ

In love there are two things — bodies and words.

— JOYCE CAROL OATES

The two divinest things this world has got,
A lovely woman in a rural spot.

—LEIGH HUNT

There are two times when a man will lie very still.
When he is finished making love with a woman.
When he is finished with life.

—MIKE ROSCOE

Sex and money are the two all-dominant motives for murder,
and of the two I'll lay odds on money every time.

—ANTHONY BOUCHER

Women complain about sex more often than men. Their gripes
fall into two major categories: (1) Not enough, (2) Too much.

—ANN LANDERS

There are two things I like stiff, and one of them's Jell-O.

—Dame Nellie Melba

There are two things that will be believed of any man whatsoever, and one of them is that he has taken to drink.

—Booth Tarkington

There are two great rules of life: never tell everything at once.

— Ken Venturi

We may divide thinkers into those who think for themselves, and those who think through others. The latter are the rule, and the former the exception.

—Arthur Schopenhauer

There are two ways to slide easily through life: to believe everything
or to doubt everything; both ways save us from thinking.

— ALFRED KORZYBSKI

Nature gave men two ends — one to sit on and one to think with.
Ever since then man's success or failure has been dependent
on the one he used most.

— GEORGE R. KIRKPATRICK

Two sorts of writers possess genius:
those who think and those who cause others to think.

— JOSEPH ROUX

Two kinds of people: . . . those who think and those who don't;
the difference comes almost entirely from education.

— JEAN-JACQUES ROUSSEAU

My grandfather believed there are two kinds of people —
those who know how the world fits together and those who think they know.
The former work in hardware stores, the latter in politics.

— JOSEF ANDERSON

A politician divides mankind into two classes: tools and enemies.

—FRIEDRICH NIETZSCHE

There are only two things in politics that matter—
money, and I can't remember the other.

—MARK HANNA

The two requisites for political leadership:
that a man know himself and that he also know his times.

—ATTRIBUTED TO BENJAMIN DISRAELI

There are two problems in my life. The political ones are insoluble
and the economic ones are incomprehensible.

—SIR ALEC DOUGLAS-HOME

You will only be remembered for two things:
the problems you solve or the ones you create.

— MIKE MURDOCK

Writers have two main problems. One is writer's block, when the
words won't come at all, and the other is logorrhea, when the words
come so fast that they can hardly get to the wastebasket in time.

— CECILIA BARTHOLOMEW

There are two literary maladies—writer's cramp and swelled head.
The worst of writer's cramp is that it is never cured;
the worst of swelled head is that it never kills.

— COULSON KERNAHAN

People who write for a living recognize only two states of being:
writing and making excuses.

— SUSAN OHANIAN

The writer of any work, and particularly any nonfiction work,
must decide two crucial points: what to put in and what to leave out.

— ANNIE DILLARD

I think there are two subtle gauges of culture:
one is architecture and the second is language.

— SUSANNA MOORE

The function of language is twofold:
to communicate emotion and to give information.

— ALDOUS HUXLEY

There are two barriers that often prevent communication between
the young and their elders. The first is middle-aged forgetfulness
of the fact that they themselves are no longer young. The second is
youthful ignorance of the fact that the middle aged are still alive.

— JESSAMYN WEST

The two greatest stimulants in the world are youth and debt.

— BENJAMIN DISRAELI

There are but two ways of paying debt — increase of industry
in raising income, increase of thrift in laying it out.

— THOMAS CARLYLE

There are two ways of meeting difficulties:
you alter the difficulties or you alter yourself to meet them.

— PHYLLIS BOTTOME

There are two ways of contending, by law and by force: the first is
proper to men; the second to beasts; but because many times
the first is insufficient, recourse must be had to the second.

— NICCOLO MACHIAVELLI

There are two primary ways to lie: to conceal and to falsify.

— Paul Ekman

There are two major kinds of promises in politics:
the promises made by candidates to the voters and the promises made by
the candidates to persons and groups able to deliver the vote. Promises
falling into the latter category are loosely called "patronage," and
promises falling into the former category are most frequently called "lies."

— Dick Gregory

Always divide people into two groups. Those who live
by what they know to be a lie, and those who live
by what they believe, falsely, to be the truth.

— Christopher Hampton

There are only two ways of telling the complete truth—
anonymously and posthumously.

—THOMAS SOWELL

The world is too dangerous for anything but truth
and too small for anything but love.

—WILLIAM SLOAN COFFIN

Two sorts of truth: trivialities, where opposites are obviously absurd,
and profound truths, recognized by the fact that the opposite
is also a profound truth.

—NIELS BOHR

Truth and love are two of the most powerful things in the world;
and when they both go together they cannot easily be withstood.

—RALPH CUDWORTH

There have existed, in every age and every country, two distinct orders of men — the lovers of freedom and the devoted advocates of power.

— ROBERT YOUNG HAYNE

There are only two powers in the world, the sword and the pen; and in the end the former is always conquered by the latter.

— NAPOLEON BONAPARTE

The two most engaging powers of an author, are, to make new things familiar, and familiar things new.

— SAMUEL JOHNSON

There are two kinds of fools: one says, "This is old, therefore it is good"; the other says, "This is new, therefore it is better."

— W. R. INGE

The Japanese . . . have a saying that there are two kinds of fool:
those who have never climbed Mount Fuji,
and those who have climbed it more than once.

—JOHN MORRIS

There are two fools in this world. One is the millionaire who thinks that
by hoarding money he can somehow accumulate real power, and the other
is the penniless reformer who thinks that if only he can take the money
from one class and give it to another, all the world's ills will be cured.

—HENRY FORD

There's only two things that money can't buy—
that's true love and home-grown tomatoes.

—GUY CLARK

Success is loving well and being loved. That's it.

—ANNA CHAVEZ

The two leading recipes for success are
building a better mousetrap and finding a bigger loophole.

— EDGAR A. SCHOAFF

There are two kinds of success — initial and ultimate.

— WINSTON CHURCHILL

There are only two dangers for a writer: success and failure,
and you have to be able to survive both.

— EDWARD ALBEE

There are two ways of exerting one's strength:
one is pushing down, the other is pulling up.

— BOOKER T. WASHINGTON

The strongest of all warriors are these two — Time and Patience.

— LEO TOLSTOY

Energy and patience in business are two indispensable elements of success.

— P. T. BARNUM

There are two cardinal sins from which all the others spring;
impatience and laziness.

— FRANZ KAFKA

There are two kinds of men who never amount to much:
those who cannot do what they are told and those who can do nothing else.

— CYRUS CURTIS

The philosophy behind much advertising is based
on the old observation that every man is really two men —
the man he is and the man he wants to be.

— WILLIAM FEATHER

I only like two kinds of men: domestic and foreign.

—ATTRIBUTED TO MAE WEST

Philosophy is concerned with two matters: soluble questions
that are trivial and critical questions that are insoluble.

—STEPHEN KANFER

There are two parts to acting: one is that you put yourself in
particular situations, where are you, what are you doing?
And then there's the other part that pertains to character,
and that's *who* are you, and *how* do you do what you're doing?

—LINDA HUNT

There are only two questions to ask about food.
Is it good? And is it authentic?

—GIULIANO BUGIALLI

In what ways do people differ from one another? There are two answers to this question. First of all, everyone has a different—and, yes, even unique—size foot. . . . The second thing that distinguishes you, sets you apart from the crowd, is that everybody in the entire world likes his eggs done a different and special way.

—FRAN LEBOWITZ

Life's two Great Questions: "Why me?" and "What do I do *now*?"

—WILLIAM L. DEANDREA

There are only two ways to live your life. One is as though nothing is a miracle. The other is as though everything is a miracle.

—ALBERT EINSTEIN

There are two things to aim at in life; first is to get what you want, and, after that, to enjoy it. Only the wisest of mankind achieve the second.

—LOGAN PEARSALL SMITH

More than any other time in history, mankind faces a crossroads. One path leads to despair and utter hopelessness. The other, to total extinction. Let us pray we have the wisdom to choose correctly.

— WOODY ALLEN

Hegel remarks somewhere that all facts and personages of great importance in world history occur, as it were, twice. He forgot to add: the first time as tragedy, the second as farce.

— KARL MARX

Events in the past may be roughly divided into those which probably never happened and those which do not matter. That is what makes the trade of historian so attractive.

— W. R. INGE

The mystery story is two stories in one: the story of what happened and the story of what appeared to happen.

— MARY ROBERTS RINEHART

Delicacy—a sad, false delicacy—robs literature of the best two things among its belongings: family-circle narrative and obscene stories.

— MARK TWAIN

There are only two families in the world, my old grandmother
used to say, the *Haves* and the *Have-nots*.

— MIGUEL DE CERVANTES

Corruption and golf is two things we might just as well
make up our minds to take up, for they are both going to be with us.

— WILL ROGERS

Golf . . . combines two favorite American pastimes:
taking long walks and hitting things with a stick.

— P. J. O'ROURKE

There are only two kinds of coaches —
those who have been fired and those who will be fired.

— KEN LOEFFLER

Football combines the two worst things about America:
it is violence punctuated by committee meetings.

— GEORGE F. WILL

Sometimes I get the feeling that the two biggest problems
in America today are making ends meet—and making meetings end.

— ROBERT ORBEN

100 The problem of education is twofold: first to know, and then to utter.
Everyone who lives any semblance of an inner life thinks
more nobly and profoundly than he speaks.

— ROBERT LOUIS STEVENSON

Every man who rises above the common level has received
two educations: the first from his teachers; the second more personal
and important, from himself.

— EDWARD GIBBON

Experience ought to teach us two things:
first, that we should do a great deal of correcting;
secondly, that we must not correct too much.

—ATTRIBUTED TO EUGÈNE DELACROIX

The essential qualities of all good teachers—
enthusiasm and the ability to convey it to others.

—ERIC HEBBORN

But there are roughly two sorts of informed people, aren't there?
People who start off right by observing the pitfalls and mistakes and
going round them, and the people who fall into them and get out and
know they're there because of that. They both come to the same
conclusions but they don't have quite the same point of view.

—MARGERY ALLINGHAM

Calamities are of two kinds:
Misfortune to ourselves, and good fortune to others.

—AMBROSE BIERCE

Ah, trouble, trouble, there are the two different kinds . . .
there's the one you give and the other you take.

—KAY BOYLE

There are two kinds of trouble:
The kind you have and the kind you haven't.
There are but few of the first sort, but of the second there is no end.

—SOPHIE IRENE LOEB

Remember, there are only two kinds of computer users: those who *have*
lost data in a crash, and those who *will* lose data in a crash.

—BOB LeVITUS

From the data, covering over a hundred shark encounters with many varieties, I can offer two conclusions: the better acquainted we become with sharks, the less we know them, and one can never tell what a shark is going to do.

— JACQUES-YVES COUSTEAU

What is the size of the world? It seems to me now that it comes in two sizes. One is exactly as big as our lives: the accumulation—precious, astonishing—of all the places we have been, all the people we have encountered, all we have touched, smelled, tasted, heard, seen. The other is the size of our longing, the immeasurable circumference of our dreams.

— DONALD GEORGE

The world seems to be divided into two groups of people: those who say you can never get something for nothing, and those muddled but happy creatures who maintain that the best things in life are free.

— JANET GILLESPIE

There are two kinds of politeness; one says, "See how polite I am";
the other, "I would make you happy."

— CHARLES TOMLINSON

I learned to distinguish between the two kinds of people in the world:
those who have known inescapable sorrow and those who have not.

— PEARL S. BUCK

There are, broadly speaking, two kinds of workers in the world,
the people who do all the work, and the people who think
they do all the work. The latter class is generally the busiest,
the former never has time to be busy.

— STELLA BENSON

There are two kinds of people in the world:
those who live poor on a lot and those who live rich on a little.

— MARCELENE COX

There are, I sometimes think, only two sorts of people in this world—the settled and the nomad—and there is a natural antipathy between them, whatever the land to which they may belong.

— FREYA STARK

A good traveler has no fixed plans and is not intent on arriving.

— LAO TZU

There are two kinds of adventurers: those who go truly hoping to find adventure and those who go secretly hoping they don't.

— WILLIAM LEAST HEAT-MOON

Nobody ought to wear a Greek fisherman's cap
who doesn't meet two qualifications:
1. He is Greek.   2. He is a fisherman.

— ROY BLOUNT, JR.

There are two sentences inscribed upon the Delphic Oracle . . .
"Know thyself" and "Nothing too much" —
and upon these all other precepts depend.

— PLUTARCH

We have, in fact, two kinds of morality side by side: one which we preach
but do not practice, and another which we practice but seldom preach.

— BERTRAND RUSSELL

Perhaps all human progress stems from the tension
between two basic drives: to have just what everyone else has
and to have what no one has.

— JUDITH STONE

Every normal young man treasures two illusions —
one, he's a good driver, and two, he's a good lover.

— ERICH FROMM

Two of the most important treasures anyone can find in life, are, one, something which can effectively take your mind off yourself and, two, something which can put you to sleep when the nighttime is your adversary. For $17.95 *The Baseball Encyclopedia* does both and consequently, dollar for dollar, it is the most valuable object ever devised by man.

—THOMAS GIFFORD

We are divided into two categories of people:
those of us who are trying to escape from something,
and those of us who are trying to find something.

—Ileana, Princess of Romania

Always remember there are two types of people in the world.
Those who come into a room and say, "Well, here I am!"
and those who come in and say, "Ah, there you are!"

—Frederick L. Collins

The longer I practice medicine, the more convinced I am
there are only two types of cases: those that involve
taking the trousers off and those that don't.

—Alan Bennett

The world is divided into two classes—invalids and nurses.

—James McNeill Whistler

The best of all medicines are resting and fasting.

— BENJAMIN FRANKLIN

The human species, according to the best theory I can form of it,
is composed of two distinct races, the men who borrow,
and the men who lend.

— CHARLES LAMB

The twin elements of a life lived intelligently are fidelity and spontaneity.

— EDWARD HOAGLAND

There is two things in life for which we are never fully prepared,
and that is twins.

— JOSH BILLINGS

There are two good things in life, freedom of thought and freedom of action.

— W. SOMERSET MAUGHAM

There are only two ways to preserve your freedom and individuality:
saying *no*, and living alone.

— NICOLAS DE CHAMFORT

Two possibilities exist: either we are alone in the universe or we are not.
Both are equally terrifying.

— ARTHUR C. CLARKE

Two forces rule the universe: light and gravity.

— SIMONE WEIL

There are two kinds of light —
the glow that illumines, and the glare that obscures.

— JAMES THURBER

There are two ways of spreading light: to be
The candle or the mirror that reflects it.

— EDITH WHARTON

I forget who it was that recommended men for their soul's good to do
each day two things they disliked: . . . it is a precept that I have followed
scrupulously; for every day I have got up and I have gone to bed.

— W. SOMERSET MAUGHAM

There are only two sure means of forgetfulness known to man —
work and drink — and, of the two, work is the more economical.

— ROBERT LYND

Kid, don't ever forget two things I'm going to tell you. One, don't believe
everything that's written about you. Two, don't pick up too many checks.

— BABE RUTH

There are two things that you've got to know about this business.
One is that it's not a done deal until the check clears.
And the other is that no news is no news.

— DOROTHY PITTMAN, ON BOOK PUBLISHING

All you need to run a news division is common sense
and a good deal of concern for humanity.

— EDWARD R. MURROW

You've only gotta do two things in this business: get it right, and be fair.

— DAVID BURGIN, ON NEWS REPORTING

There are two things one should never do after fifty:
change wives and give interviews.

— CARLOS FUENTES

At our age, we have to be careful of two things —
not to become fat physically and not to become fat mentally.

— SHIMON PERES, AT AGE SEVENTY

Character is the result of two things:
Mental attitude and the way we spend our time.

— ELBERT HUBBARD

There are two kinds of worries — those you can do something about
and those you can't. Don't spend any time on the latter.

— DUKE ELLINGTON

There are two days in the week on which I never worry:
one is yesterday and the other is tomorrow.

— ATTRIBUTED TO ROBERT JONES BURDETTE

On earth, two things are simple: relating the past and predicting the future. To see clearly from day to day is quite another thing.

— ARMAND SALACROU

There are but two roads that lead to an important goal and to the doing of great things: strength and perseverance.

— JOHANN WOLFGANG VON GOETHE

The greatest results in life are usually attained by simple means and the exercise of ordinary qualities. These may for the most part be summed up in these two—common sense and perseverance.

— OWEN FELTHAM

Because its purpose is to create a customer, the business enterprise has two—and only these two—basic functions: marketing and innovation. Marketing and innovation produce results; all the rest are "costs."

— PETER DRUCKER

There are two possible outcomes: If the result confirms the hypothesis,
then you've made a measurement. If the result is contrary
to the hypothesis, then you've made a discovery.

— ENRICO FERMI

There are, strictly speaking, only two possible fall-back positions—
prone and supine.

— PETER BOWLER

There are, I have discovered, two kinds of people in this world,
those who long to be understood and those who long to be misunderstood.
It is the irony of life that neither is gratified.

— CARL VAN VECHTEN

You see, in this world there's two kinds of people, my friend:
those with loaded guns, and those who dig. You dig.

— AGENORE INCROCCI

Work is of two kinds: first, altering the position of matter
at or near the earth's surface relatively to other such matter;
second, telling other people to do so.

—BERTRAND RUSSELL

Science has always promised two things not necessarily related—
an increase first in our powers, second in our happiness or wisdom,
and we have come to realize that it is the first and less important
of the two promises which it has kept most abundantly.

—JOSEPH WOOD KRUTCH

We may divide the struggles of the human race into two chapters:
first, the fight to get leisure; and second, what to do with our leisure
when we have won it. Like all blessings,
leisure is a bad thing unless it is well used.

—JAMES A. GARFIELD

While the battles the British fight may differ in the widest possible ways, they have invariably to common characteristics: they are always fought uphill and always at the junction of two or more map sheets.

—WILLIAM JOSEPH, VISCOUNT SLIM

Winning is overemphasized.
The only time it is really important is in surgery and war.

—AL MCGUIRE

A competitive world has two possibilities for you.
You can lose. Or, if you want to win, you can change.

—LESTER C. THUROW

There are only two possible approaches to dealing with upsetting circumstances. One is to change the circumstances; the other is to change the mind which is experiencing the upset.

—W. TIMOTHY GALLWEY

There are two principles inherent in the very nature of things —
the spirit of change, and the spirit of conservation.
There can be nothing real without both.

—ALFRED NORTH WHITEHEAD

There are two great antagonistic principles at the root
of all government — stability and experiment.

—JOHN WILSON CROKER

There are two periods when Congress does no business:
one is before the holidays, and the other after.

—GEORGE DENNISON PRENTICE

In the business world, everyone is paid in two coins: cash and experience.
Take the experience first; the cash will come later.

—HAROLD GENEEN

There are two times in a man's life when he should not speculate:
when he can't afford it, and when he can.

— MARK TWAIN

Everybody's got two businesses, his own, and show biz.

— MIKE TODD

Two of the cruelest, most primitive punishments our town deals out to
those who fall from favor are the empty mailbox and the silent telephone.

— HEDDA HOPPER, ON HOLLYWOOD

Business is a combination of war and sport.

— ANDRÉ MAUROIS

There are two things which will always be very difficult
for a democratic nation: to start a war and to end it.

— ALEXIS DE TOCQUEVILLE

There are two very difficult things in the world. One is
to make a name for oneself and the other is to keep it.

— ROBERT SCHUMANN

There are only two qualities in the world: efficiency and inefficiency;
and only two sorts of people: the efficient and the inefficient.

— GEORGE BERNARD SHAW

Two dangers constantly threaten the world: order and disorder.

— PAUL VALÉRY

When written in Chinese, the word *crisis* is composed of two characters—
one represents danger and the other represents opportunity.

—JOHN F. KENNEDY

The best index to a person's character is (a) how he treats people who can't do him any good, and (b) how he treats people who can't fight back.

—ABIGAIL VAN BUREN

There are two reasons why a man does anything. There's a good reason and there's the real reason.

—J. P. MORGAN

In life, one must show character and kindness.

—PABLO CASALS

Life is mostly froth and bubble,
Two things stand like stone,
Kindness in another's trouble,
Courage in your own.

—ADAM LINDSAY GORDON

There are two insults which no human will endure:
the assertion that he hasn't a sense of humor, and
the doubly impertinent assertion that he has never known trouble.

— SINCLAIR LEWIS

Two things, well considered, would prevent many quarrels;
first to have it well ascertained whether we are not disputing
about terms rather than things; and secondly, to examine
whether that on which we differ is worth contending about.

— CHARLES CALEB COLTON

I sometimes think that the saving grace of America lies in the fact that
the overwhelming majority of Americans are possessed of
two great qualities — a sense of humor and a sense of proportion.

— FRANKLIN D. ROOSEVELT

There are two kinds of comedy. One involves putting people down, having fun at their expense. The other recognizes that each of our lives is equally absurd.

— DONALD MONTWILL

Comedy's risky because of two reasons: one, nobody really knows *why* anything is funny; and, two, because everybody thinks he or she has a great sense of humor.

— BUCK HENRY

There are two reasons for attending a benefit. Either you believe in the cause or your arm is being twisted socially.

— ROBERT WOOLLEY

As far as I'm concerned there are only two reasons for having a husband: to carve large slabs of roasted meat and to be with you the first ten minutes of a cocktail party.

— MARY GORDON

There are two things needed in these days;
first, for rich men to find out how poor men live;
and second, for poor men to know how rich men work.

—E. ATKINSON

There are two sorts of clients: those who are already big and rich
and those who would dearly love to be big and rich.

—HOWARD GOSSAGE, ON AD AGENCY CLIENTS

In the main there are two sorts of books; those that no one reads,
and those that no one ought to read.

—H. L. MENCKEN

The two biggest sellers in any bookstore are the cookbooks
and the diet books. The cookbooks tell you how to prepare
the food and the diet books tell you how not to eat any of it.

—ANDY ROONEY

Every anthology has two types of readers:
the critics, who judge the book by what is *not* included in it, and
the general readers, who read the book for what it actually contains.

—ATTRIBUTED TO JONATHAN GRIFFIN

Let us read and let us dance—
two amusements that will never do any harm to the world.

—VOLTAIRE

Fashion constantly begins and ends in the two things it abhors most—
singularity and vulgarity.

—WILLIAM HAZLITT

There are only two emotions in a plane, boredom and terror.

—ORSON WELLES

There are two kinds of imperialists—imperialists and bloody imperialists.

—REBECCA WEST

There are two kinds of statistics, the kind you look up
and the kind you make up.

—REX STOUT

There are two kinds of pedestrians . . . the quick and the dead.

—LORD THOMAS ROBERT DEWAR

There are two kinds of people, those who finish what they start and so on.

—ROBERT BYRNE

There are two kinds of people, those who live for their outsides
and those who live for their insides.

—FRANCESCA BENDEKE

There are two kinds of people in one's life:
people whom one keeps waiting, and people for whom one waits.

—S. N. BEHRMAN

There's two kinds of people in the world, the ones who need to be told
and the ones who figure it out all by themselves.

—TOM CLANCY

There're two kinds of people—those who think there are
two kinds of people and those who have more sense.

—JAMES TIPTREE, JR.

In a consumer society there are inevitably two kinds of slaves:
the prisoners of addiction and the prisoners of envy.

—IVAN ILLICH

The two most intriguing things you can say to any reporter
worth the ink in his pen is that he may have to go to jail
if he doesn't give up his source, and that his life is in danger.

— BRIAN MCGRORY

There are only two places in our world where time takes precedence
over the job to be done: school and prison.

— WILLIAM GLASSER

There are two things that one must get used to or one will find
life unendurable: the damages of time and injustices of men.

— NICOLAS DE CHAMFORT

There are two tragedies in life. One is not to get your heart's desire.
The other is to get it.

— GEORGE BERNARD SHAW

There are two worlds: the world that we can measure with line and rule,
and the world that we feel with our hearts and imagination.

— LEIGH HUNT

The desire to understand the world and the desire to reform it
are the two great engines of progress.

— BERTRAND RUSSELL

In this world there are only two ways of getting on —
either by one's own industry or by the stupidity of others.

— JEAN DE LA BRUYÈRE

Only two things are infinite, the universe and human stupidity,
and I'm not so sure about the former.

— ALBERT EINSTEIN

The two most common elements in the known universe
are hydrogen and stupidity.

— Harlan Ellison, on would-be censors

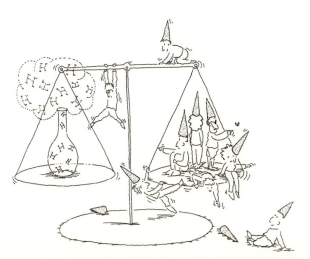

Now, there are two ways to approach a subject that frightens you and makes you feel stupid: you can embrace it with humility and an open mind, or you can ridicule it mercilessly.

— JUDITH STONE

There are two ways of seeing objects, one being simply to see them, and the other to consider them attentively.

— NICOLAS POUSSIN

There are two ways of thinking about painting, how not to do it and how to do it: *how to do it*—with much drawing and little color; *how not to do it*—with much color and little drawing.

— VINCENT VAN GOGH

Luck and destiny are the excuses of the world's failures.

— HENRY FORD

There are two ways to leave something in bad grace.
Either you leave saying, "Those rotten bastards!"
or you leave saying, "Oh, what a failure I am."

— PETER NORTON

Human beings are unique in two ways.
Man is a tool-bearing animal and a talkative animal.

— FREDERICK BODMER

People who complain about their income tax seem to
fall into two groups. Men and Women.

— BARRY R. STEINER

The world is divided into two groups of nations—those which want
to expel the Jews and those which do not want to receive them.

— CHAIM WEIZMANN

The developed world divides people neatly into two camps: those who get nervous when they have too much money on them (in case they lose it or get mugged), and those who get nervous when they don't have enough (in case they miss a bargain).

— IAIN BANKS

The world still consists of two clearly divided groups: the English and the foreigners. One group consists of less than 50 million people; the other of 3,950 million. The latter group does not really count.

— GEORGE MIKES

The world is divided into those who want to become someone and those who want to accomplish something.

— JEAN MONNET

Mankind is divisible into two great classes: hosts and guests.

— SIR MAX BEERBOHM

It is absurd to divide people into good and bad.
People are either charming or tedious.

— OSCAR WILDE

Two things are bad for the heart —
running uphill and running down people.

— BERNARD GIMBEL

There are two things in ordinary conversation
which ordinary people dislike — information and wit.

— STEPHEN LEACOCK

Wherever people foregather, one hears two kinds of talk:
that which, by and large, can be called English;
and that which is essentially gibberish.

— JOHN SIMON

There are two kinds of people who blow
    through life like a breeze,
And one kind is gossipers, and the other kind
    is gossipees.

— ODGEN NASH

I'm two things that can never be ridiculous — a child and a savage.

— PAUL GAUGIN

My father advised me that life itself was a crap game:
    it was one of the two lessons I learned as a child.
The other was that overturning a rock was apt to reveal a rattlesnake.
As lessons go those two seem to hold up, but not to apply.

— JOAN DIDION

THREES

Three has never been to me just a number.
It has always been an imperative of sorts.

—Laurens van der Post

To me travel is a triple delight:
anticipation, performance, and recollection.

—Ilka Chase

Travel is fatal to prejudice, bigotry, and narrow-mindedness.

—Mark Twain

Three simple guidelines for success in the world of travel journalism:
Be a good photographer; shoot intelligently to get good coverage;
don't be a jerk.

—Robert Holmes

There are three wants which can never be satisfied: that of the rich
wanting more, that of the sick wanting something different,
and that of the traveller who says, "anywhere but here."

—Ralph Waldo Emerson

Happiness is:
racing along in a chariot
on a dark night
toward an unknown destination.

— HENRY JAMES

The three most lethal words in a traveller's lexicon are
"you never know."

— GERALD NACHMAN, ON PACKING FOR A TRIP

The three most important words in the English language:
"Wait a minute."

— SAM RAYBURN

The three most beautiful words in the English language:
"We the people."

— BENAZIR BHUTTO

The most beautiful words in the English language are
"You've lost weight."

—CHRISTOPHER BUCKLEY

My three least favorite words are "I don't care."

—JAMES CAAN

The most moving form of praise I receive from readers
can be summed up in three words: *I never knew*.
Meaning, I see these people (call them Indians,
Filipinos, Koreans, Chinese) around me all the time
and I never knew they had an inner life.

—BHARATI MUKHERJEE

In three words I can sum up everything I've learned about life. It goes on.

—ROBERT FROST

Three words tell the whole story: *need, speed,* and *greed.*

—THOMAS HOVING, ON WHY ART EXPERTS
GET FOOLED BY FAKES

These are the three most important words to remember when you're being deposed . . . *I—don't—know.*

—WILLIAM BERNHARDT

Reason's whole pleasure, all the joys of sense, be in three words: health, peace, and competence.

—ALEXANDER POPE

Only reason can convince us of those three fundamental truths without a recognition of which there can be no effective liberty: that what we believe is not necessarily true; that what we like is not necessarily good; and that all questions are open.

— CLIVE BELL

The Japanese concept of "a knight without reproach" is composed of three imperatives: One always speaks the truth; One never lacks courage; One weeps easily.

— LAURENS VAN DER POST

I believe that it is better to tell the truth than to lie.
I believe that it is better to be free that to be a slave.
And I believe that it is better to know than to be ignorant.

— H. L. MENCKEN

There are three parts in truth: first, the inquiry, which is the wooing
of it; secondly, the knowledge of it, which is the presence of it;
and thirdly, the belief, which is the enjoyment of it.

— FRANCIS BACON

Every great scientific truth goes through three stages. First, people say
it conflicts with the Bible. Next, they say it has been discovered before.
Lastly, they say they have always believed it.

— LOUIS AGASSIZ

Science in general can be considered a technique with which
fallible men try to outwit their own human propensities
to fear the truth, to avoid it, to distort it.

— ABRAHAM MASLOW

The three basic definitions of science:

If it's green or wiggles, it's biology.

If it stinks, it's chemistry.

If it doesn't work, it's physics.

—Timothy J. Rolfe

Music can be made anywhere, is invisible and doesn't smell.

—W. H. AUDEN

Only a fool argues with a skunk, a mule or the cook.

—HARRY OLIVER

To be a good cook you have to have a love of the good,
a love of hand work, and a love of creating.

—JULIA CHILD

Culinary aphrodisiacs share three things in common:
(1) they have a large body of literature, (2) they evoke great faith
on the part of desperate people, and (3) their supposed effects
are based on very little scientifically controlled data.

—GEORGE LANG

All the things I really like to do are either immoral, illegal or fattening.
— ALEXANDER WOOLLCOTT

Sleep, riches, and health, to be truly enjoyed, must be interrupted.
— JEAN PAUL FRIEDRICH RICHTER

The things which . . . are esteemed as the greatest good of all . . . can be reduced to three headings: Riches, Fame, and Pleasure. With these the mind is so engrossed that it can scarcely think of any other good.
— BENEDICT SPINOZA

There are only three ways by which any individual can get wealth — by work, by gift, or by theft. And clearly the reason why the workers get so little is that the beggars and thieves get so much.
— HENRY GEORGE

Wealth may be an excellent thing, for it means power,
it means leisure, it means liberty.

— JAMES RUSSELL LOWELL

In every negotiation, three crucial elements are always present —
information, time, and power.

— HERB COHEN

The true delicacies are raw: oysters, salmon, and power.

— PAAVO HAAVIKKO

They had three things which the English public never forgive:
youth, power, and enthusiasm.

— OSCAR WILDE, ON BYRON, KEATS, AND SHELLEY

There are three periods in life: youth, middle age,
and "how well you look."

— NELSON ROCKEFELLER

There are only three things that can kill a farmer:
lightning, rolling over in a tractor and old age.

— BILL BRYSON

There exist only three beings worthy of respect:
the priest, the soldier, the poet. To know, to kill, to create.

— CHARLES BAUDELAIRE

There are only three ways to deal with a blackmailer. . . . You can pay
him and pay him and pay him until you're penniless. . . . You can
turn him over to the police, prosecute him, put him in prison,
and let your secret be known to the world. Or you can kill him.

— HENRY GEORGE

Folks are serious about three things —
their religion, their family, and most of all, their money.

— BERT LANCE

The three things people worry about the most are time, dirt and money.

— OLIVE ANN BURNS

To go to war three things must be ready:
money, money, and once again money.

— GIAN GIACOMO DI TRIVULZIO

To be accurate, write; to remember, write;
to know thine own mind, write.

— MARTIN FARQUHAR TUPPER

Three things in human life are important. The first is to be kind.
The second is to be kind. And the third is to be kind.

— HENRY JAMES

The three great qualities of the French writer . . .
first of all, clarity, then again clarity, and lastly, clarity.

— ANATOLE FRANCE

The things required for prosperous labor,
prosperous manufactures, and prosperous commerce are three.
First, liberty; second, liberty; third, liberty.

— HENRY WARD BEECHER

Patience. Patience. Patience! the first, and last,
and the middle virtue of a politician.

— JOHN ADAMS

Dancing is just discovery, discovery, discovery.

— MARTHA GRAHAM

To succeed as a conjurer, three things are essential —
first, dexterity; second, dexterity; and third, dexterity.

— ROBERT HOUDIN

The three most important factors in making love are:
first, opportunity; second, opportunity; third, opportunity.

— MICHEL EGUYEM DE MONTAIGNE

There are three things which the public will always clamour for,
sooner or later: namely, novelty, novelty, novelty.

— THOMAS HOOD

Three things make you a winner in this business.
Timing. Timing. And, of course, timing.

—HARRY BENSON, ON PHOTOJOURNALISM

There are three typical causes of disaster of which we should all be aware. First of these is the confusion of purpose. A second cause of possible disaster lies in overgenerous investment. A third cause of disaster results from a mistake in timing.

— C. NORTHCOTE PARKINSON

The only sensible ends of literature are, first, the pleasurable toil of writing; second, the gratification of one's family and friends; and, lastly, the solid cash.

— NATHANIEL HAWTHORNE

There are three reasons for becoming a writer: the first is that you need the money: the second is that you have something to say that you think the world should know; the third is that you can't think what to do with the long winter evenings.

— QUENTIN CRISP

There are three difficulties in authorship: to write anything
worth publishing, to find honest men to publish it,
and to get sensible men to read it.

— CHARLES CALEB COLTON

Three characteristics a work of fiction must possess in order to
be successful: (1) It must have a precise and suspenseful plot,
(2) The author must feel a passionate urge to write it,
3) He must have the conviction, or at least the illusion,
that he is the only one who can handle this particular theme.

— ISAAC BASHEVIS SINGER

Popcorn, a can of beer, and a good book is just about
as good a combination as there is in this lifetime.

— PAUL NEWMAN

A well-contrived play, like a good novel, can be told in three minutes.
One minute for the subject, one for action and plot,
and one for the denouement.

—VICTOR SARDOU

You need three things in the theatre—the play, the actors
and the audience, and each must give something.

—KENNETH HAIGH

The best audience is one that is intelligent,
well educated—and a little drunk.

—ALBEN W. BARKLEY

There are three primal urges in human beings:
food, sex and rewriting someone else's play.

—ROMULUS LINNEY

The most important things to do in this world are to get something to eat, something to drink and somebody to love you.

— BRENDAN BEHAN

Three passions, simple but overwhelmingly strong, have governed my life: the longing for love, the search for knowledge, and unbearable pity for the suffering of mankind.

—BERTRAND RUSSELL

There are three ways you can live life . . . as though it's all a cosmic accident; or you can go out at night and look at the stars and think, yes, they were created by a prime mover, and so were you, but he's aloof perfection, impassable, indifferent to his creation. . . . Then there's a third way: to live as though you believe that the power behind the universe is a power of love.

—MADELEINE L'ENGLE

There are three possible parts to a date, of which at least two must be offered: entertainment, food, and affection. It is customary to begin a series of dates with a great deal of entertainment, a moderate amount of food, and the merest suggestion of affection. As the amount of affection increases, the entertainment can be reduced proportionately. When the affection IS the entertainment, we no longer call it dating. Under no circumstances can the food be omitted.

— JUDITH MARTIN

The grand essentials of happiness are: something to do, something to love and something to hope for.

— ALLAN K. CHALMERS

Warning signs that your lover is bored: (1) Passionless kisses; (2) Frequent sighing; (3) Moved, left no forwarding address.

— MATT GROENING

Sexuality has the potential to involve three things:
the intimacy of connecting with a loved partner; the pleasures
of the body, and the satisfactions of exploring fantasy.

— DAVID WALLIN

The vine bears three kinds of grapes: the first of pleasure,
the next of intoxication, and the third of disgust.

— ANACHARSIS

There are three kinds of people —
commonplace men, remarkable men, and lunatics.

— MARK TWAIN

There are three kinds of lies. Lies, damned lies, and statistics.

— BENJAMIN DISRAELI

There are three kinds of criticism: that which has importance, that which has less importance, that which has no importance. The two last kinds don't exist; all criticism has importance.

— ERIK SATIE

There are three kinds of economist. Those who can count and those who can't.

— EDDIE GEORGE

Three kinds of progress are significant: progress in knowledge and technology, progress in the socialization of man, progress in spirituality. The last is the most important.

— ALBERT SCHWEITZER

Success depends on three things: who says it, what he says, how he says it; and of these three things, what he says is the least important.

— JOHN, VISCOUNT MORLEY

The three most important qualities to look for in a prospective member
of an expedition: loyalty, unselfishness, and dependability.

—ATTRIBUTED TO ADMIRAL ROBERT E. PEARY

There are three things, after all, that a poem must reach: the eye,
the ear, and what we may call the heart or the mind. It is the
most important of all to reach the heart of the reader.

—ROBERT FROST

I learned three important things in college—to use a library,
to memorize quickly and visually, to drop asleep at any time
given a horizontal surface and fifteen minutes.

—AGNES DE MILLE

I find that the three major administrative problems on a campus are:
sex for the students, athletics for the alumni, and parking for the faculty.

—CLARK KERR

The three best things about teaching are June, July, and August.

—ATTRIBUTED TO BILL KANE

I have tried to teach people that there are three kicks in every dollar:
one when you make it —and how I love to make a dollar;
two, when you have it—and I have the Yankee lust for saving.
The third kick is when you give it away—and it is the biggest kick of all.

— WILLIAM ALLEN WHITE

There are three ingredients in the good life:
learning, earning, and yearning.

— CHRISTOPHER MORLEY

A diplomat's life is made up of three ingredients:
protocol, Geritol and alcohol.

— ADLAI STEVENSON

Everything in life matters and ultimately has a place,
an impact and a meaning.

— LAURENS VAN DER POST

To change one's life:
- Start immediately.
- Do it flamboyantly.
- No exceptions.

— WILLIAM JAMES

Only in growth, reform and change, paradoxically enough,
is true security to be found.

— ANNE MORROW LINDBERGH

To live in this world
you must be able
to do three things:
to love what is mortal;
to hold it
against your bones knowing
your own life depends on it;
and, when the time comes to let it go,
to let it go.

— MARY OLIVER

There's just three things I'd ever say: If anything goes bad,
I did it. If anything goes semi-good, then we did it.
If anything goes real good, then you did it.
That's all it takes to get people to win football games for you.

— PAUL "BEAR" BRYANT

For a war to be just three things are necessary—
public authority, just cause, right motive.

—SAINT THOMAS AQUINAS

Three things are known only in three places: Valor, which knows
itself only in war; Wisdom, only in anger; and Friendship, only in need.

—RALPH WALDO EMERSON

When someone is wounded—first give sympathy, then first aid,
then combat negativity and loss of hope with assertions of creativity.

—ANAÏS NIN

There are three forms of visual art: painting is art to look at,
sculpture is art you can walk around, and
architecture is art you can walk through.

—DAN RICE

The artist spends the first part of his life with the dead,
the second with the living, and the third with himself.

— PABLO PICASSO

The three Gs that help the con artist most:
greed, gullibility, and goodness.

— GREG LYON

Good advertising involves intelligence,
humanity and a little bit of surprise.

— JEFF GOODBY

The true-blue virtues that won the West:
durability, honesty, and native intelligence.

— FRANK CAPRA

The credo that won the west:
straight talk, bold action, and rough justice.

—ATTRIBUTED TO PATRICK RITTER

Armaments, universal debt, and planned obsolescence—
those are the three pillars of Western prosperity.

—ALDOUS HUXLEY

It is extremely easy to convince the Swiss to violate banking secrets;
all you have to do is satisfy three conditions:
(1) Have an income of around $1 billion a year, after taxes.
(2) Have the unconditional support of a legitimate, sovereign
government whose foreign debt is close to zero.
(3) Give the Swiss a really good reason.

—PAUL-LOUP SULITZER

There are three reasons why I don't want to be a man:
(1) I don't want to open champagne, (2) I don't want to get drafted,
(3) people expect you to know something about cars.

— MARTHA WESTON

The three major expenses in life are: cars, chiropractors and psychiatrists.

— TOM & RAY MAGLIOZZI

The three major sources of apartments are death, divorce and transfer.

— CORNELIUS GALLAGHER

There are only three events in a man's life: birth, life, and death; he is not
conscious of being born, he dies in pain, and he forgets to live.

— JEAN DE LA BRUYÈRE

There's only three things for sure: taxes, death, and trouble.

—MARVIN GAYE

The most stressful experiences that one can engage in are death, weddings, and bathing suit shopping.

—SUZANNE WILDE

He had the three great requisites for a matador: courage, skill in his profession, and grace in the presence of the danger of death.

—ERNEST HEMINGWAY

Success is that old ABC—ability, breaks and courage.

—CHARLES LUCKMAN

If A is success in life, then A equals X plus Y plus Z.
Work is X; Y is play; and Z is keeping your mouth shut.

—ALBERT EINSTEIN

Three things are needed for success in painting and sculpture:
to see beauty when young and accustom oneself to it, to work hard,
and to obtain good advice.

— GIANLORENZO BERNINI

Rise early. Work late. Strike oil.

— ATTRIBUTED TO J. PAUL GETTY, FORMULA FOR SUCCESS

1. Find out how much they got.   2. Git it.   3. Git!

— W. C. FIELDS, FORMULA TO SELF-ADVANCEMENT

Hit hard, hit fast, hit often.

— WILLIAM F. HALSEY, JR., FORMULA FOR WAGING WAR

A ship under sail, a man in complete armour, and a woman with a big belly, are the three handsomest sights in the world.

— James Howell

Do you know what the three most exciting sounds in the world are? Anchor chains, plane motors, and train whistles.

— Albert Hackett and Frances Goodrich

I suspect that if my grandfather, who died a century ago, returned to Earth, the three things that would surprise him the most would be telecommunications, inflation, and the drastic shrinkage of our vocabulary. The rest was largely foreseen by Jules Verne.

— John Train

Ours is the age of substitutes: instead of language, we have jargon; instead of principles, slogans; and, instead of genuine ideas, bright ideas.

— ERIC BENTLEY

Loving kindness, warm hearts, and a stretched-out hand of tolerance — all the shining gifts that make peace on earth.

— ROBERT E. SHERWOOD AND LEONARDO BERCOVICI

Providence requires three things of us before it will help us — a stout heart, a strong arm, and a stiff upper lip.

— THOMAS CHANDLER HALIBURTON

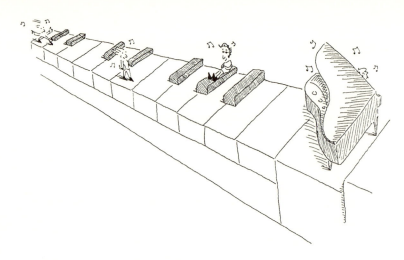

If you arrive early, you're neurotic; if you arrive on time,
you're compulsive; if you arrive late, you're hostile.

—ATTRIBUTED TO KAY HANNAH, ON PERSONALITY TRAITS
OF PIANO STUDENTS

In a world where the time it takes to travel (supersonic) or to bake a potato (microwave) or to process a million calculations (microchip) shrinks inexorably, only three things have remained constant and unrushed: the nine months it takes to have a baby, the nine months it takes to untangle a credit card dispute, and the nine months it takes to publish a hardcover book.

—ANDREW TOBIAS

Great nations write their autobiographies in three manuscripts— the book of their deeds, the book of their words, and the book of their art.

—JOHN RUSKIN

Three things make up a nation: its land, its people and its laws.

—ABRAHAM LINCOLN

There are three persons you should never deceive:
your physician, your confessor, and your lawyer.

— HORACE WALPOLE

There are times not to flirt. When you're sick.
When you're with children. When you're on the witness stand.

— JOYCE JILLSON

If you're strong on the facts and weak on the law, discuss the facts.
If you're strong on the law and weak on the facts, discuss the law.
If you're weak on the law and weak on the facts — bang on the table.

— ATTRIBUTED TO JUSTICE HARLAN FISKE STONE

Every story has three sides to it — yours, mine and the facts.

— FOSTER MEHARNY RUSSELL

Ideally, couples need three lives; one for him,
one for her, and one for them together.

— JACQUELINE BISSET

You don't marry one person; you marry three: the person
you think they are, the person they are, and the person
they are going to become as the result of being married to you.

— RICHARD NEEDHAM

Every man has three characters: the one he shows,
the one he has, and the one he thinks he has.

— ALPHONSE KARR

There are three marks of superior man: being virtuous,
he is free from anxiety; being wise, he is free from perplexity;
being brave, he is free from fear.

— CONFUCIUS

I was brought up to believe that a gentleman appears in the papers three times: when he is born, when he gets married, and when he dies. With good behaviour—and a little bit of luck—that can be managed even today.

— MICHAEL LINDSAY-HOGG

There are three things I was born with in this world,
and there are three things I will have until the day I die:
hope, determination, and song.

— MIRIAM MAKEBA

Words can be beautiful. So can dreams. So can hopes.

— F. CLIFTON WHITE

My policy is to learn from the past, focus on the present,
and dream about the future.

— DONALD TRUMP

When I was a graduate student at Harvard, I learned about showers and central heating. Ten years later, I learned about breakfast meetings. These are America's three great contributions to civilization.

— MERVYN A. KING

Never answer a telephone that rings before breakfast. It is sure to be one of three types of persons: a strange man in Minneapolis who has been up all night and is phoning collect; a salesman who wants to come over and demonstrate a combination dictaphone and music box that also cleans rugs; or a woman out of one's past.

— JAMES THURBER

Eat breakfast like a king, lunch like a prince, and dinner like a pauper.

— ADELLE DAVIS, ON EATING RIGHT

Never eat at a place called Mom's. Never play cards with
a man named Doc. And never lie down with a woman
who's got more troubles than you.

— NELSON ALGREN

In order that people may be happy in their work, these three things
are needed: they must be fit for it, they must not do too much of it,
and they must have a sense of success in it.

— JOHN RUSKIN

Work spares us from three great evils: boredom, vice and poverty.

— VOLTAIRE

There are no secrets to success. It is the result of preparation,
hard work, learning from failure.

— COLIN POWELL

The three great essentials to achieve anything worthwhile are first, hard work; second, stick-to-itiveness; third, common sense.

—THOMAS EDISON

In dealing with the press do yourself a favor. Stick with one of three responses: (a) I know and I can tell you. (b) I know and I can't tell you. (c) I don't know.

—DAN RATHER

There are three ways to get something done: do it yourself, hire someone, or forbid your kids to do it.

—MONTA CRANE

Long ago I had learned that in conversation with an irate senior, a junior should confine himself to the three remarks, "Yes, sir," "No, sir" and "Sorry, sir." Repeated in the proper sequence, they will get him through the most difficult interview with the minimum discomfort.

—WILLIAM JOSEPH, VISCOUNT SLIM

Be sincere; be brief; be seated.

—FRANKLIN D. ROOSEVELT, ON PUBLIC SPEAKING

All politicians should have three hats—one to throw into the ring,
one to talk through, and one to pull rabbits out of if elected.

—CARL SANDBURG

There are three things a woman can make out of almost anything—
a salad, a hat, and a quarrel.

—JOHN BARRYMORE

Haute Couture should be fun, foolish and almost unwearable.

— CHRISTIAN LACROIX

(1) Only iron some things, (2) Only iron the front of things,
(3) Don't iron things while you are wearing them.

— JIM DOUGLAS, TIPS ON IRONING

I believe that all people should have warm clothing, sufficient food
and adequate shelter. I do feel, however, that unless they are willing
to behave in an acceptable manner they should bundle up,
chow down, and stay home.

— FRAN LEBOWITZ

There are three things you just can't do in life.

You can't beat
the phone company

you can't make a waiter see you
until he's ready to see you,

and you can't go home again.

— BILL BRYSON

Three things only are well done in haste: flying from the plague,
escaping quarrels, and catching flies.

—H. G. Bohn

There are three things to do in dealing with a crisis—
search for the guilty, punish the innocent, promote the incompetent.

—Louis Goldman

Every revolution faces three questions. First, what to do with the king.
Second, what to do with his courtiers. And third and by far
the most difficult, what to do with people's frustrated expectations.

—Wiktor Osiatynski

He who would do good to another must do it in minute particulars:
general good is the plea of the scoundrel, hypocrite and flatterer.

— WILLIAM BLAKE

Only kings, editors, and people with tapeworm
have the right to use the editorial "we."

— MARK TWAIN

We discovered that apartments came in three varieties:
sad apartments that no one would want; interesting apartments that
would require *grands projets* to make them work; and nice apartments
that had a long private history or, to put it another way, a catch.

—ADAM GOPNIK, ON PARIS APARTMENTS

The greatest discoveries of surgery are anesthesia, asepsis and roentonology—and none was discovered by a surgeon.

—MARTIN HENRY FISHER

The three permissible excuses for *typing* a note of condolence: paralytic stroke, severed tendons, and amputation.

—ANNE TYLER

There are only three things which make life worth living: to be writing a tolerably good book, to be in a dinner party of six, and to be travelling south with someone whom your conscience permits you to love.

—CYRIL CONNOLLY

There are three roads to ruin: women, gambling, and technicians. The most pleasant is with women, the quickest is with gambling, but the surest is with technicians.

—GEORGES POMPIDOU

There are only three things to be done with a woman. You can love her, you can suffer for her, or you can turn her into literature.

— LAURENCE DURRELL

There are three things not worth running for — a bus, a woman, or a new economic panacea; if you wait a bit another one will come along.

— DEREK HEATHCOAT-AMORY

There are three intolerable things in life — cold coffee, luke-warm champagne, and overexcited women.

— ORSON WELLES

Life is very simple: it merely consists in learning how to accept the impossible, how to do without the indispensable, how to endure the insupportable.

— KATHLEEN NORRIS

For me, the big chore is always the same:
how to begin a sentence, how to continue it, how to complete it.

— CLAUDE SIMON, ON WRITING

There are three infinities: the infinitely big,
the infinitely small, and the infinitely complex.

— TEILHARD DE CHARDIN

There are three means of believing,
by inspiration, by reason, and by custom.

— BLAISE PASCAL

There are three kinds of intelligence—
the intelligence of man, the intelligence of animals,
and the intelligence of the military, in that order.

— GOTTFRIED REINHARDT

There are three great things in the world:
there is religion, there is science, and there is gossip.

— ROBERT FROST

There are three things I always forget.
Names, faces and—the third I can't remember.

— ITALO SVEVO

There are three ways in Washington to deal with embarrassing political situations. The best way is to admit them. "When I make a mistake, it's a beaut!" Fiorello La Guardia, former Mayor of New York, once said, disarming his critics. The next best way is to proclaim that your blunders were really triumphs. That wonderful old former Republican Senator from Vermont, George Aiken, advised President Johnson during the Vietnam War, "Say you won and get out!" Mr. Johnson ignored him and regretted it till the end of his days. The worst way is to pretend and blame everything that goes wrong on somebody else.

— JAMES RESTON

The three hardest tasks in the world are neither physical feats nor intellectual achievements, but moral acts: to return love for hate, to include the excluded, and to say, "I was wrong."

— SYDNEY J. HARRIS

The waste of fine tea by incompetent manipulation is considered one of the three most deplorable acts in the world—the other two being false education of youth and uninformed admiration of fine paintings.

—ATTRIBUTED TO SEN-NO RIKYU

What are the three great American things?
Jazz, the Bill of Rights, and Mark Twain.

—ROY BLOUNT, JR.

Race prejudice, class prejudice, religious prejudice, are three great forces to which the politician may appeal successfully.

—J. H. WALLIS

One can say that three pre-eminent qualities are decisive for the politician: passion, a feeling of responsibility, and a sense of proportion.

—MAX WEBER

There are three things you cannot hide:

love,

smoke,

and a man riding on a camel.

—ATTRIBUTED TO W. SCOTT DARLING

A person I knew used to divide human beings into three categories:
those who prefer having nothing to hide rather than being obliged
to lie, those who prefer lying to having nothing to hide,
and finally those who like both lying and the hidden.

— ALBERT CAMUS

Pitchers have three categories of enemies — owners, umpires and batters.

— GEORGE F. WILL

Inanimate objects are classified scientifically into three major categories —
those that don't work, those that break down, and those that get lost.

— RUSSELL BAKER

Broadly speaking, human beings may be divided into three classes:
those who are billed to death, those who are worried to death
and those who are bored to death.

— WINSTON CHURCHILL

History may be divided into three movements: what moves rapidly,
what moves slowly and what appears not to move at all.

— FERNAND BRAUDEL

All Gaul is divided into three parts:
igneous, metamorphic, and sedimentary.

— WILSON HINCKLEY, GEOLOGIST

Mr. Max Beerbohm attempted to analyze the jokes at which
the mob laughs. He divided them into three sections:
jokes about bodily humiliation, jokes about things alien,
such as foreigners, and jokes about bad cheese.

—G. K. CHESTERTON

Never bear more than one trouble at a time. Some people bear three
kinds: all they have had, all they have now, and all they expect to have.

—EDWARD EVERETT HALE

Three guidelines for Bureaucrats: (1) When in charge ponder.
(2) When in trouble delegate. (3) When in doubt mumble.

—JAMES H. BOREN

Government bureaucrats are by nature sluggish, secretive, and suspicious —
the three Ss of their craft.

— B. Atkinson

Imagination, industry, and intelligence — "the three *I*s" —
are all indispensable to the actress, but of these three
the greatest is, without doubt, imagination.

— Ellen Terry

Before Keynes there were only three great economists — Adam Smith,
who believed that God was behind economics; Ricardo, who believed
that the devil was behind them; and Karl Marx, who believed
they took it in turns but that the devil was on top at the moment.

— Lord Pakenham

There are three kinds of films:

films you want to see,

films you don't want to see,

and films you wait until they're out on video.

— ROGER EBERT

There are basically three kinds of films:
writer's films, cameraman's films, and editor's films.

— TOM PRIESTLY

If a man and a woman go into the wood with a picnic basket
and a blanket and have a picnic, that's a G. If they go into the woods
with a picnic basket and crawl under the blanket, that's a PG.
And if they go into the woods without a basket or a blanket
and have a picnic anyway, that's an R.

— JANE FONDA, ON MOVIE RATINGS

Give the angels the good looks, the devils the best lines,
and keep the prose cinematic.

— R. Z. SHEPPARD, ON WRITING POPULAR FICTION
LIKE MARIO PUZO

FOURS

Four's the only number
that romanced me . . .

—HANS OSTRUM

The four most all-American words: "Hi, Mom, I'm home!"

— BILL BRYSON

"I told you so" . . .
the four most satisfying words in the English language.

— RICHARD RUSSO

For of all sad words of tongue or pen,
The saddest are these: "It might have been!"

— JOHN GREENLEAF WHITTIER

Of all sad words on land or sea,
The saddest are these: "It could not be!"

— JAMES THURBER

Of all mean words this tongue doth know
The meanest of these is "I told you so."

— KATHARINE S. WHITE

Of all cold words of tongue or pen
The worst are these: "I knew him when—"

— ARTHUR GUITERMAN

Conversation would be vastly improved by
the constant use of four simple words: *I do not know.*

— ANDRÉ MAUROIS

What do you want, Joe, my life history?
Here it is in four words: big ideas, small results.

— ALFRED HAYES

In the Eskimo language there are four future tenses:
the immediate future, the middle future, the far-in-the-future future
and a future that will never arrive.

— ROBERT LITTELL

There are four sides to every issue: your side, my side,
the right side and the United Nations' side.

— GERALD SEGAL

An Englishman thinks seated; a Frenchman, standing;
an American, pacing; an Irishman, afterward.

— AUSTIN O'MALLEY

A Missourian gets used to Southerners thinking him a Yankee,
a Northerner considering him a cracker, a Westerner sneering at
his effete Easternness, and the Easterner taking him for a cowhand.

—WILLIAM LEAST HEAT-MOON

Frustrate a Frenchman, he will drink himself to death; an Irishman,
he will die of angry hypertension; a Dane, he will shoot himself;
an American, he will get drunk, shoot you, then establish a million dollar
aid program for your relatives. Then he will die of an ulcer.

—STANLEY RUBIN

The average Hollywood film star's ambition is to be admired
by an American, courted by an Italian, married to an Englishman
and have a French boyfriend.

—KATHARINE HEPBURN

In America only the successful writer is important, in France all writers are important, in England no writer is important, in Australia you have to explain what a writer is.

— GEOFFREY COTTERELL

A writer should immediately tell the reader four things:
1: Who the story is about.
2: What he is doing.
3: Where he is doing it.
4: When he is doing it.

— MADELEINE L'ENGLE

Every writer's life can be summed up, in sequence, by the Four Permanent Titles: "Great Expectations," "A Sentimental Education," "The Way of the World," and, finally, "Lost Illusions."

— ADAM GOPNIK

Our American professors like their literature clean
and cold and pure and very dead.

— SINCLAIR LEWIS

I think there are four great motives for writing. . . .
(1) Sheer egoism. . . .
(2) Aesthetic enthusiasm. . . .
(3) Historical impulse. . . . (4) Political purpose.

— GEORGE ORWELL

Good fiction reveals feeling, refines events, locates importance and,
though its methods are as mysterious as they are varied,
intensifies the experience of living our own lives.

— VINCENT CANBY

People who read me seem to be divided into four groups:
twenty-five percent like me for the right reasons; twenty-five percent
like me for the wrong reasons; twenty-five percent hate me for
the wrong reasons; twenty-five percent hate me for the right reasons.
It's that last twenty-five percent that worries me.

— ROBERT FROST

The tools I need for my work are paper, tobacco, food,
and a little whiskey.

— WILLIAM FAULKNER

I needed a drink, I needed a lot of life insurance, I needed a vacation,
I needed a home in the country. What I had was a coat, a hat and a gun.

— RAYMOND CHANDLER

The world may be divided into people that read,
people that write, people that think, and fox-hunters.

— WILLIAM SHENSTONE

Don't mess with cops, hoods, hunters, and the clergy.

—TOM MAGLIOZZI

Religions, like castles, sunsets and women, never reach
their maximum of beauty until they are touched by decay.

—H. L. MENCKEN

Age appears to be best in four things: old wood to turn;
old wine to drink; old friends to trust; old authors to read.

—SIR FRANCIS DRAKE

Don't smoke too much, drink too much, eat too much
or work too much. We're all on the road to the grave—
but there's no reason to be in the passing lane.

—ROBERT ORBEN

I have four good reasons for being an abstainer — my head is clearer, my health is better, my heart is lighter, and my purse is heavier.

— THOMAS GUTHRIE

Only Irish coffee provides in a single glass all four essential food groups: alcohol, caffeine, sugar, and fat.

— ALEX LEVINE

The four descending degrees of drunkenness: the first, that which enlivens; the second, that which irritates; the third, that which stupefies; finally the last, that which brutalizes.

— VICTOR HUGO

Men are nicotine-soaked, beer-besmirched, whiskey-greased, red-eyed devils.

— CARRY NATION

No drug, not even alcohol, caused the fundamental ills of society.
If we're looking for the source of our troubles, we shouldn't test
people for drugs, we should test them for
stupidity, ignorance, greed and love of power.

— P. J. O'ROURKE

I hate to advocate drugs, alcohol, violence, or insanity to anyone,
but they've always worked for me.

— HUNTER S. THOMPSON

Winston Churchill's habit of guzzling a quart or two a day
of good cognac is what saved civilization from the Luftwaffe,
Hegelian logic, Wagnerian love-deaths, and potato pancakes.

— CHARLES MCCABE

One drink of wine, and you act like a monkey; two drinks, and you strut like a peacock; three drinks, and you roar like a lion; and four drinks—you behave like a pig.

—HENRY VOLLAM MORTON

The first glass for myself, the second for my friends, the third for good humor, and the fourth for mine enemies.

—SIR WILLIAM TEMPLE

Pick the right grandparents, don't eat or drink too much, be circumspect in all things, and take a two-mile walk every morning before breakfast.

—HARRY S TRUMAN, ON LONGEVITY

Everyday: meditation, chocolate, a glass of port wine, and flirting with young men.

—BEATRICE WOOD, AT AGE NINETY-EIGHT, ON HER LONGEVITY SECRET

Recipe for a long life:
1. Having leisure equals power.
2. Going to bed early equals having wealth.
3. A leisurely stroll is as enjoyable as a drive.
4. Eating late is as good as eating meat.

—Su Tung-p'o

The four stages of man are infancy, childhood,
adolescence and obsolescence.

—Art Linkletter

From birth to age eighteen, a girl needs good parents.
From eighteen to thirty-five, she needs good looks.
From thirty-five to fifty-five, she needs a good personality.
From fifty-five on, she needs good cash.

—Sophie Tucker, at age sixty-nine

He that is not handsome at twenty, nor strong at thirty, nor rich at forty, nor wise at fifty, will never be handsome, strong, rich or wise.

— GEORGE HERBERT

The four virtues characteristic of great men: humility, respect for superiors, graciousness towards dependents, and a sense of justice towards subordinates.

— CONFUCIUS

The Four Virtues: Wisdom, Justice, Fortitude, and Temperance.

— MARCUS AURELIUS

Perfect wisdom hath four parts, namely, wisdom, the principle of doing things correctly; justice, the principle of doing things equally in public and private; fortitude, the principle of not fleeing danger, but meeting it; and temperance, the principle of subduing desires and living moderately.

— PLATO

The wise are instructed by reason; ordinary minds, by experience;
the stupid, by necessity; and brutes by instinct.

— Cicero

Art, if it is to be reckoned as one of the great values of life,
must teach men humility, tolerance, wisdom and magnanimity.

— W. Somerset Maugham

Painting deals with the only issues that seem to me to count
in our benighted time — freedom, autonomy, fairness, love.

— Andrew Forge

There are certain things in which mediocrity is not to be endured —
poetry, music, painting, and public speaking.

— Jean de La Bruyère

The four most beautiful things in life are thunder,
lightning, a falling star, and the roar of a lion.

—LAURENS VAN DER POST

He was an ideal sightseer, for he knew when to stop,
had friends in the city, was acquainted with the best restaurants
and thoroughly understood the first principle of aesthetic appreciation,
which is that it can usually be doubled by sitting down.

— ROBERTSON DAVIES

If one must travel, one should do it with the eyes of a child,
the mind of an ecologist, the heart of a pagan, and the words of a poet.

— KIRKPATRICK SALE

The things I remember most, for travel is all vanished remembered
stories . . . are about food, sex, music, and houses.
These things in combination are especially good.

— MICHELLE DOMINIQUE LEIGH

Civilized men arrived in the Pacific, armed with
alcohol, syphilis, trousers, and the Bible.

— HAVELOCK ELLIS

If you reject the food, ignore the customs, fear the religion
and avoid the people, you might better stay home.

— JAMES A. MICHENER, ON TRAVEL

Respect, Understanding, Caring and Fairness —
the four fundamental, universal human values that affirm
and promote the human spirit in all circumstances.

— TOM RUSK

The four fundamental things that dog all societies . . .
folly, corruption, mediocrity, and incompetence.

— STANLEY CROUCH

The vices of authority are chiefly four:
delays, corruption, roughness and facility.

— FRANCIS BACON

Competence, like truth, beauty, and contact lenses,
is in the eye of the beholder.

— LAURENCE J. PETER

220

The first ingredient in conversation is truth; the next, good sense;
the third, good humor; and the fourth, wit.

— SIR WILLIAM TEMPLE

Every new truth has its birth-place in a manger,
lives thirty years, is crucified, and then deified.

— LUCY STONE

We are afraid of truth, afraid of fortune, afraid of death
and afraid of each other.

— Ralph Waldo Emerson

There are four ways I can defend murder.
Number one, it wasn't murder, it was suicide or accidental.
Two, you didn't do it. Three, you were legally justified,
like the defense of your home or property.
Four, the killing was excusable.

— attributed to Wendell Mayes

There are four kinds of homicide: felonious, excusable, justifiable,
and praiseworthy, but it makes no great difference
to the person slain whether he fell by one kind of another—
the classification is for the advantage of lawyers.

— Ambrose Bierce

The four-level classification system for whistle-blowers:
good person/good information; bad person/good information;
good person/bad information; bad person/bad information.

— ATTRIBUTED TO DAVID DURK

In the news media, there are four conditions of discussions
between sources of information and the reporters who seek
knowledge from them . . . "on the record" . . . "on background" . . .
"deep background" . . . "off the record."

— BRIAN MCGRORY

There is, of course, a certain amount of drudgery in newspaper work,
just as there is in teaching classes, tunneling into a bank,
or being President of the United States.

— JAMES THURBER

Newspapers should come in four sections:
Truth, Probability, Possibility, and Lies.

—ATTRIBUTED TO THOMAS JEFFERSON

A gentleman's name should appear in the newspaper only four times:
when he's born, when he marries, when he's indicted, and when he dies.

—O. L. OSNAD

Such a perfect lady! She never raises her voice, she never fidgets,
she never contradicts, she never gets untidy.

—ELIZABETH BIBESCO

There are four stages in a marriage. First there's the affair,
then the marriage, then children and finally the fourth stage,
without which you cannot know a woman—the divorce.

—NORMAN MAILER

There are only four sure-fire excuses for arriving late for your own wedding: I was in an auto accident; I was held at gunpoint by robbers; I was detained by the President; and it took longer than I thought to divorce my previous wife.

—ATTRIBUTED TO DANIEL VANDELES

First there is a time when we believe everything without reasons,
then for a little while we believe with discrimination, then we believe
nothing whatever, and then we believe everything again —
and, moreover, give reasons why we believe everything.

— G. C. Lichtenberg

Four things come not back: the spoken word; the sped arrow;
time past; the neglected opportunity.

— Omar Ibn Al-Halif

I've got four things to live by: don't say nothin'
that will hurt anybody; don't give advice, nobody will take it anyway;
don't complain; don't explain.

— Walter "Death Valley Scotty" Scott

Four be the things I am wiser to know:
Idleness, sorrow, a friend, and a foe.

—DOROTHY PARKER

The four things that are good for the auction business are
death, divorce, debt, and disease.

—ROBERT WOOLLEY

Four things to look for when buying a car:
safety, durability, comfort, style.

—TOM AND RAY MAGLIOZZI

Research is four things: brains with which to think, eyes with which
to see, machines with which to measure, and fourth, money.

—ALBERT SZENT-GYÖRGYI

Of four things every man has more than he knows:
sins, debts, years, and foes.

—ARCHBISHOP RICHARD CHENEVIX TRENCH

Four things hurt the sight of all men, that is tears, smoke, wind,
and the worst of all, to see his friend unlucky and his enemies happy.

—JOHN FLORIO

Four things greater than all things are,
Women and Horses and Power and War.

—RUDYARD KIPLING

The art of war is simple enough. Find out where your enemy is.
Get at them as soon as you can. Strike at him as hard as you can,
and keep moving on.

—ULYSSES S. GRANT

This strategy would involve us in the wrong war, at the wrong place, at the wrong time, and with the wrong enemy.

—General Omar Bradley, on confronting Communist China during the Korean War

An extraordinarily gifted president who was the wrong man from the wrong place at the wrong time under the wrong circumstances.

—Eric F. Goldman, on Lyndon Johnson

Politics is the art of looking for trouble, finding it, misdiagnosing it and then misapplying the wrong remedies.

—Groucho Marx

The biggest mistake is believing there is one right way to listen, to talk, to have a conversation—or a relationship.

—Deborah Tannen

A mature person is one who does not think only in absolutes,
who is able to be objective even when deeply stirred emotionally,
who has learned that there is both good and bad in all people
and all things, and who walks humbly and deals charitably
with the circumstances of life, knowing that in this world no one
is all-knowing and therefore all of us need both love and charity.

— ELEANOR ROOSEVELT

Some American Delusions:
(1) That there is no class-consciousness in the country.
(2) That American coffee is good.
(3) That Americans are business-like.
(4) That Americans are highly sexed and that
redheads are more highly sexed than others.

— W. SOMERSET MAUGHAM

Those of us who shout the loudest about Americanism in making character assassinations are all too frequently those who, by our own words and acts, ignore some of the basic principles of Americanism—

The right to criticize.

The right to hold unpopular beliefs.

The right to protest.

The right of independent thought.

—MARGARET CHASE SMITH

The essential American soul is hard, isolate, stoic, a killer.

—D. H. LAWRENCE

There are many reasons why people get murdered,
but ninety-nine percent fall into four broad motive categories:
love, hate, greed, insanity.

—JOHN DUNNING

There is nothing wrong with America that the faith, love of freedom, intelligence, and energy of her citizens cannot cure.

— DWIGHT D. EISENHOWER

We look forward to a world founded upon four essential human freedoms. The first is freedom of speech and expression everywhere in the world. The second is freedom of every person to worship God in his own way everywhere in the world. The third is freedom from want . . . everywhere in the world. The fourth is freedom from fear . . . anywhere in the world.

— FRANKLIN D. ROOSEVELT

There are things that are worth dying for—the honor of one's country, the sanctity of the home, the virtue of women, and the safety of little children. But, if they are worth dying for, they are worth living for!

— GEORGE W. TRUETT

The soil out of which such men as he are made is good to be born on, good to live on, good to die for and to be buried in.

—JAMES RUSSELL LOWELL

In any nonviolent campaign there are four basic steps:
(1) collection of the facts to determine whether injustices are alive,
(2) negotiation, (3) self-purification, and (4) direct action.

—MARTIN LUTHER KING, JR.

Action, swiftness, violence, power: these are native, homegrown American qualities, derived from the vast continent that has been ours to open up, and the big prizes that have made our economy into a jungle where the law is eat or be eaten.

—MAX LERNER

Neither snow, nor rain, nor heat, nor gloom of night stays these couriers from the swift completion of their appointed rounds.

— HERODOTUS

1. Whom the gods would destroy, they first make mad with power.
2. The mills of God grind slowly, but the grind exceedingly small.
3. The bee fertilizes the flower it robs.
4. When it is dark enough, you can see the stars.

—CHARLES A. BEARD, BASIC LESSONS OF HISTORY

Once you're a star actor, people start asking you questions
about politics, astronomy, archaeology, and birth control.

—MARLON BRANDO

Four species of idols beset the human mind: idols of the tribe,
idols of the den, idols of the market, and idols of the theatre.

—FRANCIS BACON

Walk in, plant yourself, look the other fellow in the eye,
and tell the truth.

— JAMES CAGNEY, ON ACTING

Walk groundly, talk profoundly, drink roundly, sleep soundly.

— WILLIAM HAZLITT

The Corn Belt is a gift of the gods — the rain god, the sun god,
the ice god, and the gods of geology.

— J. RUSSELL SMITH

In Washington, the first thing people tell you is what their job is.
In Los Angeles you learn their star sign. In Houston you're told
how rich they are. And in New York they tell you what their rent is.

— SIMON HOGGART

In California we don't have seasons;
we have Earthquake, Fire, Flood, and Panic.

— HELEN HUNT

The four building blocks of the universe are
fire, water, gravel, and vinyl.

— DAVE BARRY

It isn't necessary to imagine the world ending in fire or ice —
there are two other possibilities: one is paperwork,
and the other is nostalgia.

— FRANK ZAPPA

You can feel nostalgia for things that have happened, that you wish
had happened, that happened before you were born,
and some that even happened only in your imagination.

— O. L. OSNAD

The past is what you remember, imagine you remember,
convince yourself you remember, or pretend to remember.

— GEORGE ORWELL

The field of philosophy may be reduced to the following questions:
1. What can I know? 2. What ought I do?
3. What may I hope for? 4. What is man?

— IMMANUEL KANT

I'm 42 around the chest, 42 around the waist, 96 around the golf course,
and a nuisance around the house.

— GROUCHO MARX

The ideal voice for radio should have no substance, no sex, no owner,
and a message of importance for every housewife.

— EDWARD R. MURROW

There are four warning signs of a short attention sp

—JOHN GRIMES

Order. Routine. Chaos. Joy.

—MAURICE RAVEL, MAXIM

Giggle, gabble, gobble, git.

—OLIVER WENDELL HOLMES, ON THE MAIN ACTIVITIES
AT A TEA PARTY

Live pure, speak true, right wrong, follow the King.

—ALFRED, LORD TENNYSON

Use it up. Wear it out. Make it do. Do without.

—ELEANOR ROOSEVELT

Think in the morning. Act in the noon.
Eat in the evening. Sleep in the night.

— WILLIAM BLAKE

Manifest plainness, Embrace simplicity,
Reduce Selfishness, Have few desires.

— LAO-TZU

Buy low, sell high, collect early, and pay late.

— DICK LEVIN

Promotion: new title, new salary, new office, same old crap.

— JIM FISK AND ROBERT BARRON

He said he was dying of fast women, slow horses,
crooked cards and straight whiskey.

— KENNETH REXROTH, ON HIS FATHER

A good woman inspires a man, a brilliant woman interests him,
a beautiful woman fascinates him, but a sympathetic woman gets him.

— HELEN ROWLAND

Be intellectual with pretty women, frivolous with intellectual women,
serious with young girls, and flippant with old ladies.

— GELETT BURGESS

There are four ways to write a woman's life. The woman herself may
tell it, in what she chooses to call an autobiography; she may tell it
in what she chooses to call fiction; a biographer, woman or man,
may write the woman's life in what is called a biography; or the woman
may write her own life in advance of living it, unconsciously,
and without recognizing or naming the process.

— CAROLYN G. HEILBRUN

Without books, history is silent, literature dumb,
science crippled, thought and speculation at a standstill.

— BARBARA TUCHMAN

Four things can not stay hidden for long:
Science, Stupidity, Riches, and Poverty.

— ATTRIBUTED TO HICAR

Four be the things I'd been better without:
Love, curiosity, freckles, and doubt.

— DOROTHY PARKER

Some say kissing is a sin; but if it was not lawful, lawyers would not
allow it; if it was not holy, ministers would not do it; if it was not modest,
maidens would not take it; if it was not plenty, poor folk would not get it.

— ROBERT BURNS

You're an attorney. It's your duty to lie, conceal and
distort everything and slander everybody.

— JEAN GIRAUDOUX

Lawsuits consume time, and money, and rest, and friends.

— GEORGE HERBERT

Four great moments in a mom's life—
First Communion, college graduation, the wedding,
and first adjudication on a criminal offense.

— ROBERT K. TANENBAUM

Mother, food, love, and career are the four major guilt groups.

— CATHY GUISEWITE

We never make sport of religion, politics, race or mothers.

— MACK SENNETT, ON HIS SLAPSTICK COMEDY

Disney Studios . . . has four guideline for screenplays: no snow
(winter scenes are out), no headlines (recent news stories are out),
no rural (the action must take place in an urban area),
and no dust (Westerns are out).

— IAN FRAZIER

The magician has four duties: To lie to you, deceive you, surprise you, and entertain you.

—DAN X. SOLO

There are four secrets to success on the stage: Know your lines, say them loudly, look at the audience, and never let 'em see you sweat.

— BARON EMERSON

The FBI's four touchstones for successful hostage negotiation: honesty, conciliation, containment, and resolution.

— WILLIAM BERNHARDT

The only country which any man has a right to love is one where there is a balanced judgment, justice founded on wisdom, a free spirit and a temperate mind.

— JUDGE LEARNED HAND

We surveyed our members as to what's troubling them. Number one is government. Number two is government. Number three is government and number four is government.

— RICHARD LESHER, ON THE CHAMBER OF COMMERCE

The only gracious way to accept an insult is to ignore it;
if you can't ignore it, top it; if you can't top it, laugh at it;
if you can't laugh at it, it's probably deserved.

— RUSSELL LYNES

The different branches of Arithmetic —
Ambition, Distraction, Uglification, and Derision.

— LEWIS CARROLL

You're adopted, you're sick in the head, Mom says you need
a psychiatrist, you're gonna work in a laundromat.

— ATTRIBUTED TO CYNTHIA KANE, ON THE BEST TAUNTS
TO USE ON ONE'S SIBLINGS

Honest criticism is hard to take, particularly from a relative,
a friend, an acquaintance, or a stranger.

— FRANKLIN P. JONES

At first people refuse to believe that a strange new thing can be done,
then they begin to hope it can be done, then they see it can be done—then
it is done and all the world wonders why it was not done centuries ago.

— FRANCES HODGSON BURNETT

Progress: the search for the best possible product
at the most possible mark-up with the shortest possible duration
for the earliest possible replacement.

— JOHN CIARDI

The four great motives which move men to social activity
are hunger, love, vanity, and fear of superior powers.
If we search out the causes which have moved men to war
we find them under each of these motives or interests.

— WILLIAM GRAHAM SUMNER

The opposite of love is not hate, it's indifference.
The opposite of art is not ugliness, it's indifference.
The opposite of faith is not heresy, it's indifference.
The opposite of life is not death, it's indifference.

— ELIE WIESEL

The first element of greatness is fundamental humbleness
(this should not be confused with servility); the second is freedom
from self; the third is intrepid courage, which, taken in its widest
interpretation, generally goes with truth; and the fourth—
the power to love—although I have put it last, is the rarest.

— MARGOT ASQUITH

There are four kinds of people in the world: those who love,
those who are ambitious, those who watch and imbeciles.
The happiest are the imbeciles.

— HIPPOLYTE TAINE

There are four legs to stand on. The first, be romantic.
The second, be passionate. The third, be imaginative.
And the fourth, never be rushed.

—CHARLES OLSON

The more things you love, the more you are interested in,
the more you enjoy, the more you are indignant about,
the more you have left when anything happens.

—ETHEL BARRYMORE

The four best things in life: to love, to be in love,
to be loved, and to make love.

—LILO BLOCH

The four Ls to practice each day:
Loving, Living, Learning, and Letting go.

—MARIAN M. JUNG

Acquire the art of detachment, the virtue of method, and the quality of thoroughness, but above all the grace of humility.

—SIR WILLIAM OSLER

The four most important things for the health of one's inner life are faith, hope, love—and an occasional cold to encourage humility.

—PHILIP MARTIN

Objection, evasion, distrust and irony are signs of health. Everything absolute belongs to pathology.

—FRIEDRICH NIETZSCHE

When you don't have any money, the problem is food. When you have money, it's sex. When you have both, it's health. If everything is simply jake, then you're frightened of death.

—J. P. DONLEAVY

According to the Spanish proverb, four persons are wanted
to make a good salad: a spendthrift for oil, a miser for vinegar,
a counselor for salt, and a madman to stir all up.

— ABRAHAM HAYWARD

Good manners are a combination of intelligence, education, taste,
and style mixed together so that you don't need any of those things.

— P. J. O'ROURKE

Below you will find the complete and unabridged record of the
general conversation of the general public since time immemorial:
    a. Hi, how are you?
    b. I did not.
    c. Good. Now you know how I felt.
    d. Do you mind if I go ahead of you?
       I only have this one thing.

— FRAN LEBOWITZ

Throw high risers at the chin; throw peas at the knees; throw it here when they're lookin' there; throw it there when they're lookin' here.

— SATCHEL PAIGE, ON PITCHING

The best way to treat sports injuries: rest, ice, compression, elevation.

— DICK FRANCIS

Pain is important: how we evade it, how we succumb to it, how we deal with it, how we transcend it.

— AUDRE LORDE

It is by disease that health is pleasant; by evil that good is pleasant; by hunger, satiety; by weariness, rest.

— HERACLITUS

There are only the pursued, the pursuing, the busy, and the tired.

— F. Scott Fitzgerald

Here are instructions for being a pigeon: (1) Walk around aimlessly for a while, pecking at cigarette butts and other inappropriate items. (2) Take fright at someone walking along the platform and fly off to a girder. (3) Have a shit. (4) Repeat.

— Bill Bryson

In each human heart are a tiger, a pig, an ass, and a nightingale. Diversity of character is due to their unequal activity.

— Jamrach Holobom

There is nothing in the world that is not mysterious, but the mystery
is more evident in certain things than in others: in the sea,
in the eyes of the elders, in the color yellow and in music.

— JORGE LUIS BORGES

There are only four kinds of answers to a question: the short answer,
the long answer, the answer that's known but not told, and the truth.
The first three are as close as we can come to the fourth, because
everything we believe is true is so much less than the whole truth
that really, in this life, there's only one kind of answer to any question:
the wrong answer.

— MAX GREENSTREET